Best Easy Day Hikes
Redding, California

Help Us Keep This Guide Up to Date

Every effort has been made by the author and editors to make this guide as accurate and useful as possible. However, many things can change after a guide is published—trails are rerouted, regulations change, facilities come under new management, etc.

We would love to hear from you concerning your experiences with this guide and how you feel it could be improved and kept up to date. While we may not be able to respond to all comments and suggestions, we'll take them to heart and we'll also make certain to share them with the author. Please send your comments and suggestions to the following address:

Globe Pequot Press
Reader Response/Editorial Department
P.O. Box 480
Guilford, CT 06437

Or you may e-mail us at:

editorial@GlobePequot.com

Thanks for your input, and happy trails!

Best Easy Day Hikes Series

Best Easy Day Hikes Redding, California

Montana Hodges

FALCON GUIDES

GUILFORD, CONNECTICUT
HELENA, MONTANA

AN IMPRINT OF GLOBE PEQUOT PRESS

FALCONGUIDES®

FaclonGuides is an imprint of Globe Pequot Press.

TOPO! Explorer software and SuperQuad source maps courtesy of National Geographic Maps. For information about TOPO! Explorer, TOPO!, and Nat Geo Maps products, go to www.topo.com or www .natgeomaps.com.
Maps created by James Fountain © Morris Book Publishing, LLC
Project editor: David Legere
Layout Artist: Kevin Mak

Library of Congress Cataloging-in-Publication Data is available on file.

ISBN 978-0-7627-5254-6

Printed in the United States of America
10 9 8 7 6 5 4 3 2 1

Contents

Acknowledgments viii
Introduction 1
How to Use This Guide 9
Trail Finder 11
Map Legend 13

The Hikes

1. Lassen Volcanic National Park: Bumpass Hell 14
2. Lassen Volcanic National Park: Kings Creek Falls 19
3. Lassen Volcanic National Park: Paradise Meadows 24
4. Lassen Volcanic National Park: Manzanita Lake Trail 28
5. Burney Falls Loop Trail 32
6. McCloud River Falls 37
7. Squaw Valley Creek Trail 42
8. Bunny Flat to Horse Camp 47
9. Castle Lake Trail 52
10. Castle Crags State Park: Indian Creek Nature Trail 56
11. Pacific Crest Trail to Burstarse Falls 60
12. Clikapudi Trail 65
13. Whiskeytown National Recreation Area: James K. Carr Trail (Whiskeytown Falls) 69
14. Whiskeytown National Recreation Area: Camden Water Ditch Trail 74
15. Whiskeytown National Recreation Area: Oak Bottom Water Ditch Trail 78
16. Hornbeck and Sacramento Ditch Trails 82

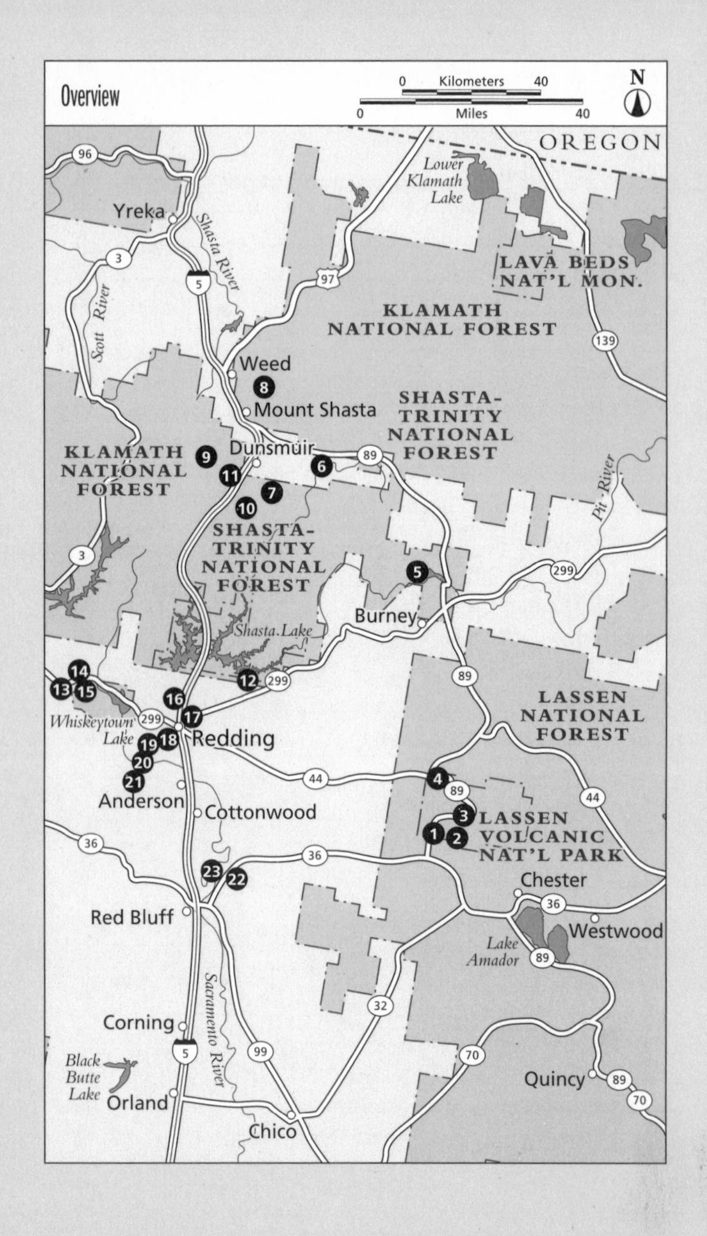
Overview
0 Kilometers 40
0 Miles 40
N
OREGON
Lower Klamath Lake
LAVA BEDS NAT'L MON.
KLAMATH NATIONAL FOREST
Yreka
Shasta River
Scott River
Weed
Mount Shasta
SHASTA-TRINITY NATIONAL FOREST
Dunsmuir
KLAMATH NATIONAL FOREST
Pit River
Burney
Shasta Lake
Whiskeytown Lake
Redding
LASSEN NATIONAL FOREST
Anderson
Cottonwood
LASSEN VOLCANIC NAT'L PARK
Chester
Westwood
Lake Amador
Red Bluff
Corning
Sacramento River
Black Butte Lake
Orland
Chico
Quincy

17. Lema Ranch and Churn Creek Trails 87
18. Sacramento River and Rail Trails 92
19. Westside Trail to Salt Creek 97
20. Wintu Trail 101
21. Clear Creek Greenway to Horsetown's Vista Point 105
22. Hog Lake Plateau 109
23. Yana Trail 113

Clubs and Trail Groups 117
About the Author 119

Acknowledgments

The biggest acknowledgment for this book goes to the many agencies that cooperatively manage Redding's public land. The City of Redding alone deserves a standing ovation for its dedication to protecting open space as well as developing land for recreational use. Dozens of other organizations have come together with the same mind-set to assemble and maintain these trails. I have been deeply inspired and impressed by the outdoor spirit of Redding and the success of these well-managed, multiuse public lands. Also a special thanks to Reddingite Arron Banowetz for guidance on the selection of these trails, as well as an enhanced perspective. Thanks, too, to hiking partners Dr. Doom, John Cooney, Chris Acosta, Julie Chinn, Thomas Adkins, and my wonderful canine cohort, Teddy. Without your company, I would have spied far fewer squirrels.

Introduction

Redding is located on the northern cusp of the Sacramento Valley, nuzzled up to the grassy foothills and further bound to the north by the magnificent merge of the Klamath Mountains and Cascade Range. With a plethora of recreational opportunities and landscapes, the region has something to offer everyone—and at every time of the year. The community of Redding has a strong outdoor-oriented culture that rallies to protect and preserve, as well as utilize, these recreational lands. Perhaps no city in California's great Central Valley has dedicated as much time, energy, and money to the development of trail systems. Most area trails are a result of the cooperative effort between public and private land managers, nonprofit organizations, grassroots organizations, and hundreds of volunteers. The urban options continue to grow each year, with a tally of around 100 miles of trails in the city alone.

The impressive array of hiking options doesn't cease at the city line, but instead crosshatches the surrounding hills and climbs high into the mountains. Down the southern lowlands of the valley, the scenic Sacramento River Parkway stretches 60 protected miles along the threatened waterway from the concrete monolith of Shasta Dam to the city of Red Bluff. Once again, a multitude of land managers joined forces to support this Sacramento River project. Nearly a million people visit the parkway each year, and it continues to grow as a preserve almost by the day. On the western outskirts of the city proper is Whiskeytown National Recreation Area, home to another 150 miles of trails. Shasta Lake sits enticingly close to the city's north end. An hour's drive from Redding will take you to awe-inspiring Mount Shasta, unique Castle Crags State Park, powerful Mount Lassen Volcanic National Park, and beautiful McArthur–Burney Falls State Historical Park, not to mention the thousands of acres of public lands between.

Climate

If you're new to the area, the summer heat can take you by surprise. Redding is subject to a Mediterranean climate, with rainy winters, occasional sprinkles of snow, and dry, very hot summers. Redding lies at an elevation around 500 feet, with a slight gain in the valley's fringing foothills. The peaks that nestle within this valley remain snowcapped all winter long but can also roast in the hot months. Summer days in the area can easily crest at over 100°F. This extreme heat is important to take into account when planning a summer hike. Even for those of us who grew up in this climate, 90°F hikes can still prove overwhelming. Never doubt how quickly dehydration and sun exposure can set in. Shade can be essential to the journey, and trails that offer relief from the scorching sun have been noted. If you hike midday in the summer months, think about trekking close to a water source, possibly with a swimming beach. Even the mountainous portions of the region won't bring much relief to extreme temperatures, however. Prepare for this heat by packing plenty of water for the journey. Pack the swimsuits, but don't forget your hat, sunblock, and SPF-added lip balm!

Wildlife

The Redding region is home to a collection of viewable wildlife, including bears, mountain lions, and rattlesnakes. Probably the biggest wildlife problem in Redding are the annoying mosquitoes and flies (always pack the bug spray, even in winter!), or the occasional cow wandering down the trail. If a cow is blocking your route, give way to the beast and change your course. Never approach any animal, even cattle. Cows, particularly mothers with calves, can be dangerous. Some of these trails cross through territory leased to ranchers who run cattle on the property. It is important when passing through gates to always close the gates behind you.

For the critters that can't be dissuaded by bug repellent and farm gates, certain precautions reduce your risk and encourage positive relationships.

Bears

There is a healthy population of black bears in the Redding region, and if you spend enough time in the outdoors, it is likely you'll come across one. Bears are curious creatures; they are attracted to odors, especially of food. They are omnivores and are constantly on the lookout for the next meal, usually of any accessible kind. To avoid bears, eliminate odors as much as possible—this means all sorts of odors, from perfume to garbage. Bears also don't like surprises. Most encounters can be avoided by taking the proper precautions and using common sense. Always make your presence known, and never put yourself in a position where you could surprise a bear. Make lots of noise. Use your voice, probably the most effective bear repellent there is.

Mountain Lions

Mountain lions, also known as cougars, but not to be confused with bobcats, are elusive felines that are not commonly seen and rarely attack humans. If you do encounter a mountain lion, stand your ground, try to appear as large as possible, and do not run. Raise your hands above your head and maintain eye contact. Use a stern voice and yell at the mountain lion. If all else fails, fight back.

Rattlesnakes

Shy creatures, rattlesnakes are not curious at all and will avoid human interaction if possible. Rattlesnakes will bite humans in defense, but their bite is rarely fatal, and most encounters prove peaceful. The best way to avoid close encounters is to watch your footing, especially in rocky areas. These cold-blooded reptiles like to warm themselves on the hot rocks or use them for shade at the hottest time of day. Look before you step, and avoid hiking over crevasses and rock piles if possible. If you hear the warning rattle, stop immediately and locate the snake, then move in the proper direction to avoid it. If you are bitten, ice the wound and immediately seek medical attention where an antivenin can be given.

Poison Oak

Poison oak is found on nearly every trail detailed in this book, and flourishes incognito with its oaklike appearance. Just one accidental swipe of a branch or a leaf, and invisible oil coats your skin. This oil is quickly transferred by touch and can cause an irritating rash that easily spreads. Study photos of poison oak in a nature guide to train yourself to recognize this tricky plant before you hit the trails. One distinguishing feature is a leaf pattern consisting of three leaves per cluster. This noticeable characteristic has led to the popular expression "Leaves of three? Let it be!" Abide by it. There are some common distinctions to look out for. During spring, poison oak also hosts a distinctive yellow flower that morphs into small grapelike clusters of green and white berries later in summer. In fall the deciduous plant changes leaf colors from dark green into beautiful shades of yellow, orange, and red. After the fall change and deep into spring, poison oak is nothing more than a naked stem. Look for the vertical reaches of gray stems, which can grow anywhere from a few inches to over a dozen feet tall, singular or in clusters—they are still toxic. This may sound like a challenge now, but once you've fallen victim to the itch, it's easy to make plant identification a priority on subsequent adventures.

Safety and Preparation

Maps

Rough maps, meant to serve as an overview of hiking locations, are included in this book. You will need to obtain more specific ones for each area you visit. Unfortunately, there is not a single map source in Redding, and it is important to contact each specific land manager in advance in regards to trail conditions and maps. You can secure maps from the BLM Redding Field Office at 355 Hemsted Dr., Redding, CA 96002 (530-224-2100); the California Welcome Center at 1699 CA 273, Anderson, CA 96007 (530-365-7500); and the Shasta Trinity National Forest Supervisors Office at 3644 Avtech Pkwy., Redding, CA 96002 (530-226-2500). Many maps are also available online. Along with these maps, be sure to bring a GPS and a compass.

Clothing

Redding is subject to hot, dry summers and cool, wet winters. The higher elevations of the foothills and mountains around the valley's perimeter see snow in the colder months. Whatever season you hike in, layering is the way to go. Layering prepares you for all sorts of weather and keeps things lightweight. Synthetic fibers are a must: Wet cotton does not wick away sweat in the hot months or insulate in winter. For the base layer choose a synthetic shirt and pants designed to pull moisture away from your body. If the weather has the potential to get chilly, you can add an insulating layer, such as fleece. The outer layer should be a waterproof shell. If you are taking a high-elevation hike, you can always add thermals under the base, along with gloves and a hat. Bring both a warm, waterproof hat and a sun hat.

Secure, comfortable, and well-fitting footwear is essential for hiking. Wandering around the wilderness with open toes or inadequate shoes could cause any number of accidents. Depending on your activity, choice of trail, and time of year, you may want hiking boots or running shoes or something in between. Whatever your level requires, in the wetter months make sure that your shoes are waterproof, or prepare for wet feet. The risk of wet feet leads to one of the most important items—socks. In winter, wool socks are best because they still insulate even if they get wet. Again, if not wool, stick with synthetics and avoid cotton at any time of year.

Survival Gear

Carry extra water on all your hikes in the Redding region. It is easy to become dehydrated while hiking, especially during the scorching summer months. Water availability at trailheads has been noted, but the status of this could change at any time. Bring the essential survival gear on your hikes outside the city, including a day pack with extra water and clothing. A good trail pack includes a water purifier, compass, bug spray, emergency blanket, pocket knife, flashlight, waterproof matches, first-aid kit, and safety whistle. Most trails in this region are well established and easy to follow, but hikers can still become lost or disoriented.

Zero Impact

Trails in the Redding area and surrounding mountains are heavily used year-round. We, as trail users and advocates, must be especially vigilant to make sure our passage leaves no lasting mark. Here are some basic guidelines for preserving trails in the region:

- Pack out all your own trash, including biodegradable items like banana peels. You might also pack out garbage left by less-considerate hikers.
- Don't approach or feed any wild creatures—the ground squirrel eyeing your snack food is best able to survive if it remains self-reliant.
- Don't pick wildflowers or gather rocks, antlers, feathers, and other treasures along the trail. Removing these items will only take away from the next hiker's experience.
- Avoid damaging trailside soils and plants by remaining on the established route. This is also a good rule of thumb for avoiding poison oak and stinging nettle, common regional trailside irritants.
- Don't cut switchbacks, which can promote erosion.

- Be courteous by not making loud noises while hiking.
- Many of these trails are multiuse, which means you'll share them with other hikers, trail runners, mountain bikers, and equestrians. Familiarize yourself with the proper trail etiquette, yielding the trail when appropriate.
- Use outhouses at trailheads or along the trail.

How to Use This Guide

This guide is designed to be simple and easy to use. Each hike includes a map and summary information that describes the trail's vital statistics, including length, difficulty, fees and permits, park hours, canine compatibility, and trail contacts. Directions to the trailhead are also provided, along with a general description of what you'll see along the way. A detailed route finder (Miles and Directions) sets forth mileages between significant landmarks along the trail.

Difficulty Ratings

These are all easy hikes, but *easy* is a relative term. To aid in the selection of a hike that suits particular needs and abilities, each is rated easy, moderate, or more challenging. Bear in mind that even the most challenging routes can be made easy by hiking within your limits and taking rests when you need them.

- **Easy** hikes are generally short and flat, taking no longer than an hour to complete.
- **Moderate** hikes involve increased distance and relatively mild changes in elevation and will take one to two hours to complete.
- **More challenging** hikes feature some steep stretches, greater distances, and generally take longer than two hours to complete.

These are completely subjective ratings—consider that what you think is easy is entirely dependent on your level of fitness and the adequacy of your gear (primarily shoes). If you are hiking with a group, you should select a hike with a rating that's appropriate for the least fit and least prepared in your party.

Approximate hiking times are based on the assumption that on flat ground, most walkers average 2 miles per hour. Adjust that rate by the steepness of the terrain and your level of fitness (subtract time if you're an aerobic animal and add time if you're hiking with kids), and you have a ballpark hiking duration. Be sure to add more time if you plan to picnic or take part in other activities, like bird-watching or photography.

Trail Finder

Best Hikes for Waterfalls

- 2 Kings Creek Falls (Lassen Volcanic National Park)
- 5 Burney Falls Loop Trail
- 6 McCloud River Falls
- 13 James K. Carr Trail (Whiskeytown Falls)

Best Hikes for Geology Lovers

- 1 Bumpass Hell (Lassen Volcanic National Park)

Best Hikes for Children

- 5 Burney Falls Loop Trail
- 6 McCloud River Falls
- 10 Indian Creek Nature Trail (Castle Crags State Park)
- 17 Lema Ranch and Churn Creek Trails
- 18 Sacramento River and Rail Trails

Best Hikes for Dogs

- 7 Squaw Valley Creek Trail
- 11 Pacific Crest Trail to Burstarse Falls
- 16 Hornbeck and Sacramento Ditch Trails
- 20 Wintu Trail
- 23 Yana Trail

Best Hikes for Great Views

- 1 Bumpass Hell (Lassen Volcanic National Park)
- 8 Bunny Flat to Horse Camp

Best Hikes for Lake Lovers

- 4 Manzanita Lake Trail (Lassen Volcanic National Park)
- 9 Castle Lake Trail

12 Clikapudi Trail

15 Oak Bottom Water Ditch Trail (Whiskeytown National Recreation Area)

Best Hikes for Nature Lovers

3 Paradise Meadows (Lassen Volcanic National Park)

7 Squaw Valley Creek Trail

8 Bunny Flat to Horse Camp

9 Castle Lake Trail

23 Yana Trail

Map Legend

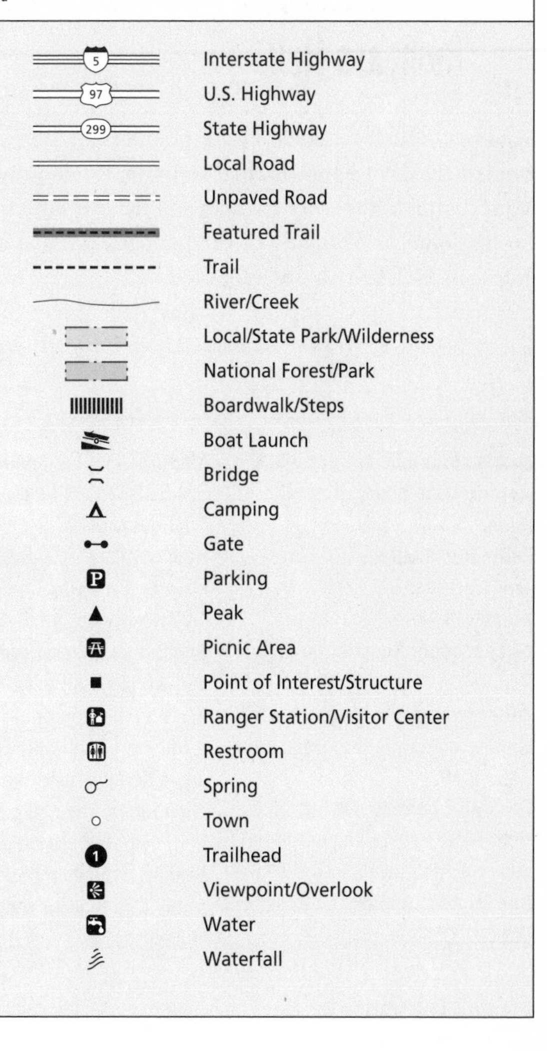
5
97
299
Interstate Highway
U.S. Highway
State Highway
Local Road
Unpaved Road
Featured Trail
Trail
River/Creek
Local/State Park/Wilderness
National Forest/Park
Boardwalk/Steps
Boat Launch
Bridge
Camping
Gate
Parking
Peak
Picnic Area
Point of Interest/Structure
Ranger Station/Visitor Center
Restroom
Spring
Town
Trailhead
Viewpoint/Overlook
Water
Waterfall

1 Lassen Volcanic National Park: Bumpass Hell

Lassen Volcanic National Park's premier hike showcases the wildest thrills of hydrothermal activity a stone's throw from your hiking boots—hot gas spewing from hissing fumaroles, boiling mud, and brightly colored mineral pools. The hike to Bumpass Hell first climbs a forested hillside ridge showcasing classic mountain vistas before its final decent into the sizzling valley below. If you only have a day in Lassen, head straight to the Hell.

Distance: 3-mile out-and-back
Approximate hiking time: 2.5 hours
Difficulty: Moderate
Trail surface: Dirt, rock, and boardwalk track
Best season: Summer through fall
Other trail users: None
Canine compatibility: Dogs not permitted
Fees and permits: Day-use fee
Schedule: Park open year-round; hike only accessible in the snow-free months, approximately June through Oct
Maps: TOPO! California CD, Disc 3; USGS Lassen Peak, CA
Trail contacts: Lassen Volcanic National Park, P.O. Box 100, Mineral, CA 96063; (530) 595-4444; www.nps.gov/lavo
Special considerations: You may be tempted to wander off this trail, but the brittle ground aside the boardwalks could prove deadly; mind the trail boundaries. The steep drop into Bumpass Hell can be a little slippery on the decomposed granite, so be sure to wear secure hiking boots.

Finding the trailhead: Lassen Volcanic National Park can be reached either from CA 44 to the north or CA 36 south through Red

Bluff. To enter the park from the north, from Redding take CA 44 about 48 miles east and turn south onto CA 89. Drive 1.6 miles to the entrance of Lassen Volcanic National Park on your right. Follow the park road 23 miles south to the Bumpass Hell trailhead/parking area just south of Lake Helen at N40 27.961' / W121 30.841'. If you enter the park from the southern entrance, you will find this trailhead on your right, 6 miles from the park's southern entrance.

The Hike

Over a hundred years ago, Lassen Volcanic National Park, was known as Cinder Cone and Lassen Peak National Monuments. It didn't take long for onlookers to recognize the geologic significance of the land, namely the eruption of Mount Lassen in 1915. The eruption was so furious, gusts of ash piercing the sky were seen from as far south as Sacramento. By 1917 the monument was bumped up to the status of a national park. The park itself is not home to just one active volcano, but instead a complex mesh of several volcanoes of different sizes, ages, and types. The great namesake, Lassen Peak, is one of the most voluminous plug volcanoes in the world.

It is Lassen's sidekick, Brokeoff Mountain, that can take credit for the prodigious sprawl known as Bumpass Hell. Brokeoff's unfathomably hot magma pooled deep below the surface has heated the bedrock and water above to scorch the small basin. The result is the boiling, screaming, colorfully denuded sixteen-acre sprawl suitably known as Bumpass Hell. No area in the park better displays the alive-and-kicking workings of this volcano, and as you tiptoe the boardwalks along this trail, there is no doubt in your mind that you are in fact balancing on the shell of an active volcano. Don't forget the camera!

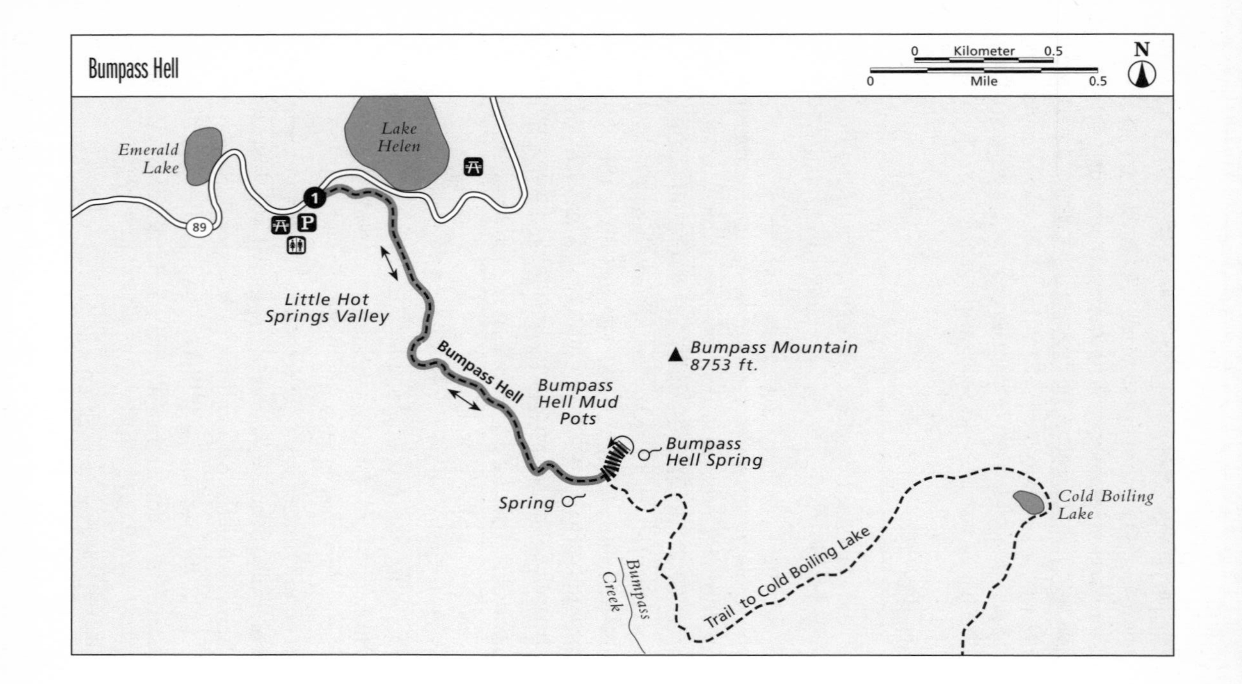
Bumpass Hell
0 Kilometer 0.5
0 Mile 0.5
N
Emerald Lake
Lake Helen
89
1
P
Little Hot Springs Valley
Bumpass Hell
Bumpass Mountain 8753 ft.
Bumpass Hell Mud Pots
Bumpass Hell Spring
Spring
Bumpass Creek
Trail to Cold Boiling Lake
Cold Boiling Lake

The trail begins a tad south of Lake Helen, at a small parking area overlooking the Little Hot Springs Valley. From there, you can pick up the route via a paved path in the northeast corner. A couple hundred feet into the forest, the footing transitions into the rocky earthen single-track path you'll follow to the Hell. The original topography of the hike says little about the scene ahead. The ridgeline ascent cuts through mature stands of pines, firs, cedars, and twisted mountain hemlocks. Lake Helen jumps into sight briefly on the left, beckoning for a later journey. Distant peaks, including Lassen, Diller and the rocky shards of Brokeoff Mountain herself, come into view as you climb an open mountainside. This mile-long portion of the hike can be spectacular in early summer when the mountainside is covered in a periwinkle blanket of silver-leaf lupines.

You will smell the roasted basin long before you finally descend into Bumpass Hell. Kids will get a kick out of the rotten-egg-like smell of sulphur gas. When you do arrive, the valley stands in stark contradiction to the evergreen forest you ascended. The dominant scene is of steaming, eerily treeless slopes covered in a colorful mosaic of soils against a backdrop of chalky white hills. It is not just the sights, or smells, that enliven Bumpass Hell, but also the sounds. One notably loud gas vent dominates all others: Big Boiler is the hottest fumarole within a nonerupting volcano in the world, skyrocketing up to 322°F. Interpretive signs mark the boardwalk and explain the geologic history, so be sure to allow plenty of time for this exciting tour.

Before the trail morphs into the boardwalks, don't pass up the opportunity to read an interpretive sign by the bench on the left for the invaluable knowledge of why this area was christened Bumpass Hell. (*Hint*: Kendall Vanhook

Bumpass began this hike with two good legs and came out with only one. Stay on the boardwalks!) What appears to be secure footing aside the trail may actually be eggshell-thin sedimentary layers crusted over scorching water, mud, or gas.

Miles and Directions

0.0 Pickup the trail at the interpretive sign in the the northeast corner of the parking area.

0.2 A small unlabeled trail to the left forks to road and Lake Helen, stay right, heading southeast, for Bumpass Hell.

1.2 Descend into Bumpass Hell where boardwalks lead to interpretive signs. For an extension you can hop on the the trail just before the boardwalk and follow signage an additional 1.9 miles one-way to Cold Boiling Lake.

1.5 The boardwalk ends.

3.0 Arrive back at the trailhead.

2 Lassen Volcanic National Park: Kings Creek Falls

This heart-healthy hike in Lassen Volcanic National Park descends along a rocky route past a meadow of summer-long wildflower blooms and a spectacularly cool creek. The hike climaxes at the ultimate summer escape: Kings Creek Falls, a multitiered giant made famous from park brochures and Lassen ad campaigns. You will surely recognize this feathery waterfall.

Distance: 2.4- or 3-mile out-and-back or 2.75-mile loop
Approximate hiking time: 2 hours
Difficulty: Moderate
Trail surface: Dirt and rock path
Best season: Summer
Other trail users: None
Canine compatibility: Dogs not permitted
Fees and permits: Day-use fee
Schedule: Park open year-round; hike only accessible in snow-free months, approximately June through October
Maps: TOPO! California CD, Disc 3; USGS Reading Peak, CA
Trail contacts: Lassen Volcanic National Park, P.O. Box 100, Mineral, CA 96063; (530) 595-4444; www.nps.gov/lavo
Special considerations: No facilities at the trailhead

Finding the trailhead: Lassen Volcanic National Park can be reached either from CA 44 to the north or CA 36 through Red Bluff from the south. To enter the park from the north, from Redding take CA 44 about 48 miles east and turn south onto CA 89. Drive 1.6 miles to the entrance of Lassen Volcanic National Park. Follow the park road south 17 miles to the parking area on your right, just across the highway from the Kings Creek Trailhead at N40 27.616' / W121 27.599'. If you enter the park from the southern entrance, you will find this trailhead on your right 13 miles north of the park's southern entrance.

The Hike

Within Lassen Volcanic National Park's 106,000 acres, there are a dozen or so well-known cascades, but none deserves the title of "king" so much as Kings Creek Falls. This thunderous waterfall showers a multitiered gorge in several crosshatching streams before crashing into a dark pool below. The poster child of the park is arguably the most beautiful waterfall in the boundaries, and it's blessedly accessible.

The hike to the falls offers two options, and the 700-foot elevation drop and subsequent gain is a force to be reckoned with. Luckily, you can spread the grade over a north-fork detour known as Horse Trail and create a moderate 3-mile round-trip hike compared to a briefer 2.4-mile option along Kings Creek. Each route offers similar charm, but the shorter track is rockier, steep, and wet. It is also possible to create a loop combining the two options. For the best compromise consider taking Horse Trail down to the falls and returning on the steeper creekside climb that parallels an unforgettable series of Kings Creek cascades. Whatever direction you opt to tour, proper footwear is essential at any time of year. Consider the uneven terrain and think about secure ankle support, gripping outsoles, and waterproof boots.

Both hikes begin in an alpine forest along Kings Creek, where you may spy deer. The waters of this brook are on their way to the Warner Valley (catch a vista of this picturesque, evergreen-blanketed valley behind you on your way up). Silverleaf lupine, fawn lily, and scarlet paintbrush add color to the creek in the summer wildflower months. After about 0.5 mile on the creek, the easier Horse Trail curves off to the north. This descent detours from the creek for a spell but saves your energy for the prize at the end.

When you meet back up with the main route, the Kings Creek parallel continues. With each step the increasingly forceful sounds of the water amplify, indicating that you are almost there. A visit in early July will show the falls in all its gushing glory, showering a cool mist around the pool, a cherry on the sundae for those hot summer escapes. In the afternoon the falls are in the shade, so if it's photographic opportunities you're after be sure to arrive at dawn. You might notice the curled trunks of the trees next to the basaltic boulders that Kings Creek Falls showers. The park brochure will explain that these giants are California red firs, mangled from the annual snowpack, when as much as 15 feet of snow weighs down their bases each winter.

Although it is hard to put the shimmering spectacle behind you, the hike is enduringly attractive on the return, especially if you choose to triumph the steeper route along the cascades—a wild rushing exposure through a slim canyon above. The shorter return parallels an extensive series of rapids along Kings Creek on a rocky, slippery track. At times, the trail traverses small boulders and weathering rock stairs. The hike levels out when the roar of the cascades gives way to the peaceful meadow. The contrast of the woods, falls, cascades and meadow completes the alpine experience of Lassen.

Miles and Directions

0.0 From the Kings Creek Falls Trailhead, head southeast on the dirt trail.

0.5 At the intersection with the Sifford Lake Trail, stay left, heading east, onto the Kings Creek Falls Trail.

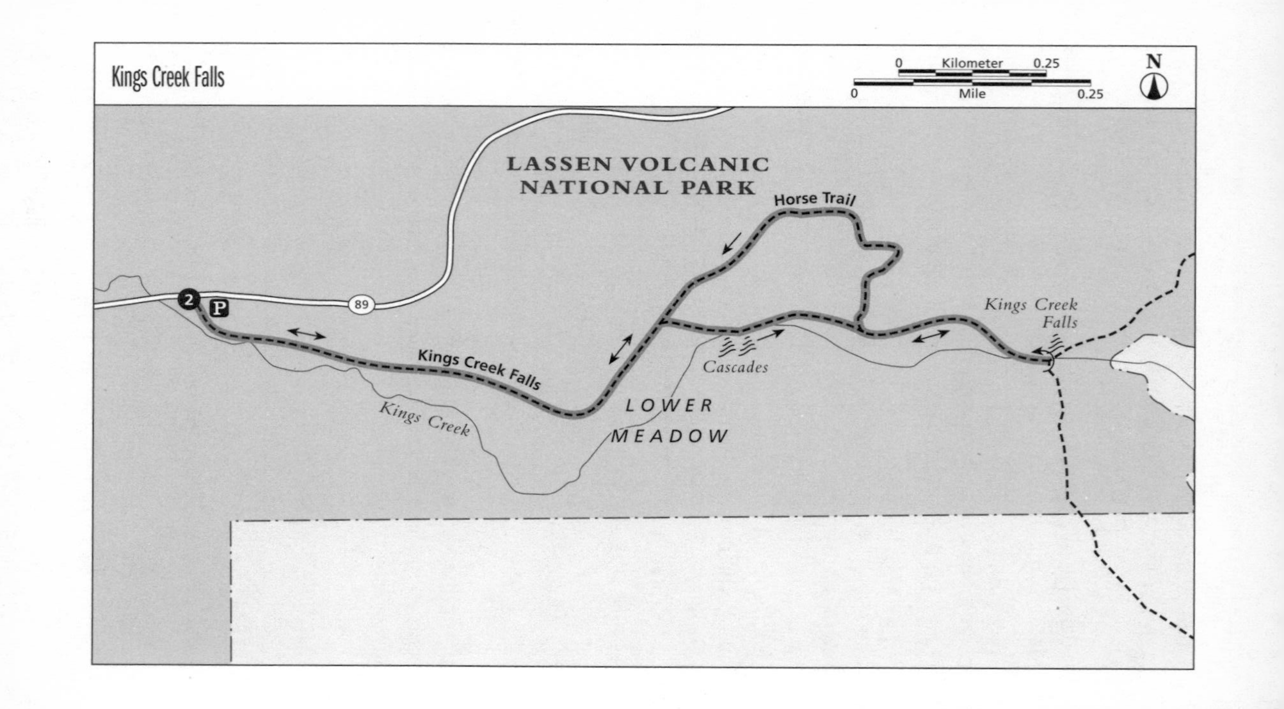
Kings Creek Falls
0
Kilometer
0.25
0
Mile
0.25
N
LASSEN VOLCANIC
NATIONAL PARK
Horse Trail
89
2
P
Kings Creek Falls
Kings Creek
Cascades
LOWER
MEADOW
Kings Creek
Falls

0.6 At the intersection with Horse Trail, go left, heading north, for the Horse Trail. The steeper more direct route to the cascades along Kings Creek heading southeast also leads to the falls.

1.3 Rejoin the Kings Creek Falls Trail. Stay left, heading southeast, for the trail to the falls.

1.4 Intersection with the trails to Sifford and Bench Lakes, stay left, heading east for Kings Creek Falls.

1.5 Reach Kings Creek Falls, backtrack from here.

1.8 At the intersection with Horse Trail, stay left, heading northwest, for Kings Creek Trail along the cascades.

2.7 Arrive back at the trailhead.

3 Lassen Volcanic National Park: Paradise Meadows

Another gem of Lassen Volcanic National Park, the Paradise Meadows hike offers a little piece of, well, paradise! Splashed in the beauty of wildflowers all summer long, the captivating meadow is framed by a rich evergreen forest and towering mountaintops. The scene brings memorable meaning to the expression "picture perfect." The rugged, 1.4-mile each-way trail is a bit steep, but it's worth every step, even when it's vertical.

Distance: 2.8-mile out-and-back
Approximate hiking time: 2 hours
Difficulty: Moderate
Trail surface: Dirt and rock single-track path
Best season: Summer
Other trail users: None
Canine compatibility: Dogs not permitted
Fees and permits: Day-use fee
Schedule: Park open year-round; hike only accessible in snow-free months, approximately June through October
Maps: TOPO! California CD, Disc 3; USGS Lassen Peak, CA
Trail contacts: Lassen Volcanic National Park, P.O. Box 100, Mineral, CA 96063; (530) 595-4444; www.nps.gov/lavo
Special considerations: No facilities at the trailhead

Finding the trailhead: Lassen Volcanic National Park can be reached either from CA 44 or CA 36 through Red Bluff. To enter the park from the north, from Redding take CA 44 about 48 miles east and turn south onto CA 89. Drive 1.6 miles and turn right at the entrance of Lassen Volcanic National Park. You'll find the parking area for this trailhead 10 miles down the park road on the left aside the Hat Lake Trailhead at N40 30.565' / W121 27.900'. You will have to cautiously cross the road from the parking area to reach the trail. If you enter the park from the southern entrance, you will find this trailhead on your left, and the parking area on your right, 20 miles from the park entrance.

The Hike

Paradise Meadows offers a different flavor of Lassen Volcanic National Park, although the trophy at the end of the footpath is just as dramatic as a towering waterfall or a boiling lake. Paradise Meadow is an unexpectedly peaceful patch of scenery tucked away among the volcanic rubble of the park. The flourishing meadow is thick with summer-long wildflowers and encompassed by healthy green forest and high mountains.

The trail doesn't get much traffic compared to other Lassen Volcanic National Park day hikes, which is a worthy trade for the less-developed route. The route is also much more rugged than other polished park trails, offering a charming taste of rustic wilderness en route to Paradise Meadow. To reach the trail from the parking area, carefully cross the park road and have a quick gander of Hat Lake. Follow the gravel path through the forest as it turns to dirt among patches of tall pine, fir, and droopy hemlock along Hat Creek. Depending on the time of year, this creek can have a decent flow or be more of a trickle. When the forests fade into willow thickets and streams, watch your footing as you cross a couple of small, rickety footbridges.

After about a mile, the climb reaches its most strenuous grade. Parallel to the rushing creek, this portion remains cool all summer long. A sharp rise up a ledge before the waterfall keeps you young, and by the time you pass the gushing fall, the trail levels out. The gradual grade up the mountainside

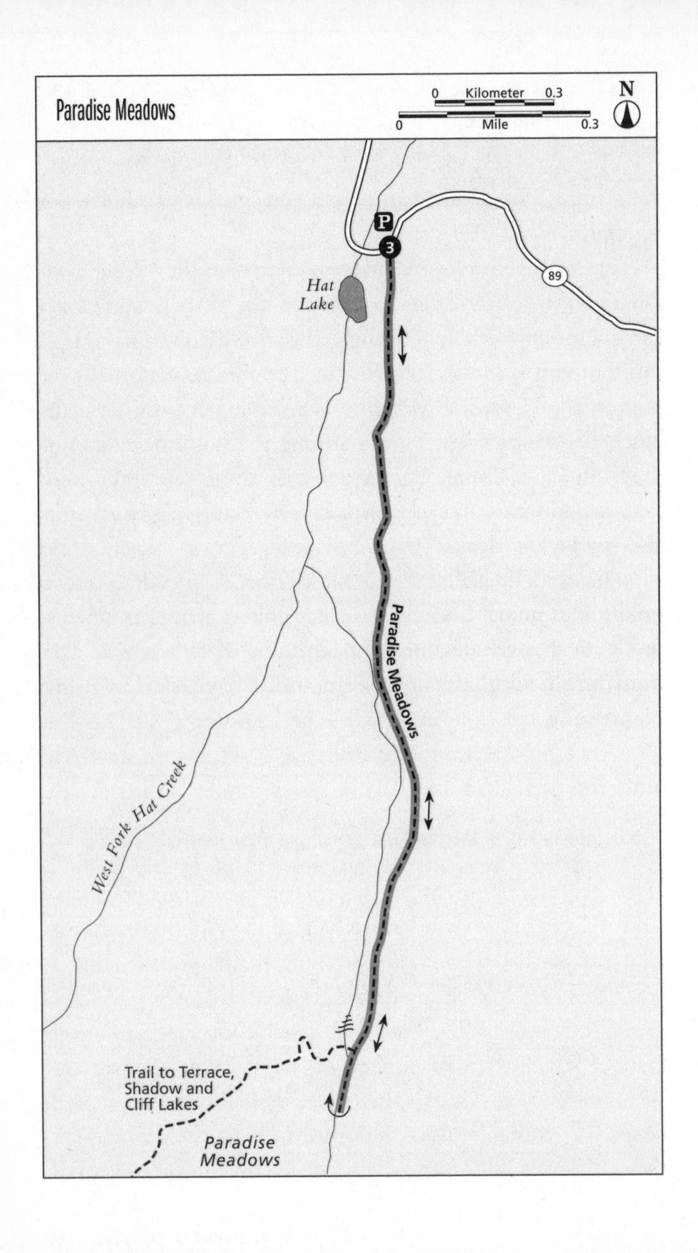

Paradise Meadows
0
Kilometer
0.3
0
Mile
0.3
N
P
3
89
Hat
Lake
Paradise Meadows
West Fork Hat Creek
Trail to Terrace,
Shadow and
Cliff Lakes
Paradise
Meadows

can be a challenging experience for some, but remember that this trail is only as hard as you make it. Wander at your own pace and stop and smell the lupine. The 20-foot triple-drop waterfall is a nice place to take a break and admire the bounty of small Hat Creek.

The trail gently drops into the meadow after the waterfall. It would be hard not to be taken back by the perfection of this vale, which looks as if it was pulled from an Ansel Adams photo. Hat Creek subtly fans out into the marshy center of the meadow, and wildflower displays are dazzling, particularly in the late summer. Over a dozen species may bloom at once, including blood red paintbrush, pink gentian, soft blue lupine, and violet penstemon. You might also spy yellow monkey flower, scarlet gilia, and dark purple monkshood. Unless it is the tail end of fall, pack along a wildflower guide. Don't have one? Grab a map-size pocket guide to Lassen wildlife at Manzanita Lake's store. The miniature field guides can distinguish the classics from the obscure.

Miles and Directions

0.0 Beginning at the Hat Lake parking area, carefully cross the park road to the trailhead and follow the gravel route south.

1.3 Arrive at the waterfall.

1.4 Reach Paradise Meadows.

2.8 Arrive back at the trailhead.

4 Lassen Volcanic National Park: Manzanita Lake Trail

This breezy stroll loops around stunning Manzanita Lake at the northern entrance of Lassen Volcanic National Park. The placid waters and mountainous backdrop offer some of the better photographic opportunities in the park, with Lassen Peak poised perfectly above the brilliantly blue lake. The Manzanita Lake Trail is a popular little 1.8-mile route, but you can catch the lake nearly all to yourself if you arrive at dawn, when it's just you and the pika.

Distance: 1.8-mile loop
Approximate hiking time: 1.5 hours
Difficulty: Easy
Trail surface: Dirt path
Best season: Spring through fall
Other trail users: None
Canine compatibility: Dogs not permitted
Fees and permits: Day-use fee
Schedule: Day use only
Maps: TOPO! California CD, Disc 3; USGS Manzanita Lake, CA
Trail contacts: Lassen Volcanic National Park, P.O. Box 100, Mineral, CA 96063; (530) 595-4444; www.nps.gov/lavo

Finding the trailhead: Lassen Volcanic National Park can be reached either from CA 44 or CA 36 through Red Bluff. To enter the park from the north, from Redding take CA 44 about 48 miles east and turn south onto CA 89. Drive 1.6 miles to the entrance of Lassen Volcanic National Park on your right. Follow the park road about 0.5 mile to the entrance station. Follow the immediate signs west to the Manzanita Lake Campground and park at the boat launch and picnic area. The main trailhead is on the south edge of the parking lot at N40 32.045' / W121 33.829'. If you enter the park from the southern entrance, you will find the trailhead 32 miles north from the southern entrance, on your left just before the northern entrance station.

The Hike

One of the dominant forces of volcanic action aside from eruptions is the aftermath of tons of debris. Chaos Crags, standing rocky and tall, are the very host for the rockfall that naturally dammed Manzanita Creek and created this aquatic stroke of good fortune. Manzanita Lake stands up to its reputation as a must-see on Lassen tours, even if the water level has been enhanced by human endeavors and the shores have become a magnet for visitors. If you enter Lassen Volcanic National Park from the north, Manzanita Lake will be the first landmark of this exciting national park. The lake, trail, and campground are practically intertwined with the Visitors Center where you can also pick up the trail. At the 200-site campground, and preferred trailhead for this route, you will find a general store, boat launch, picnic and, on a busy day, upward of a hundred people.

Pick up the trail adjacent to the amphitheater at the boat launch trailhead. If you head right onto the loop, creating a counterclockwise direction, you will save the best scenery for last and immediately enter a section of the trail unfortunately wedged around activity. As soon as you put the Visitors Center behind you, CA 89 comes up on your right and follows your tour for around a 0.25 mile. But once you swing a sharp left along the shoreline just after the entrance station, you can look great distances without seeing anything man-made and morph back into a nature vibe.

Surprisingly, it is easy to find peace on this placid lake. The quiet shores attract a fairly quiet crowd (most of the

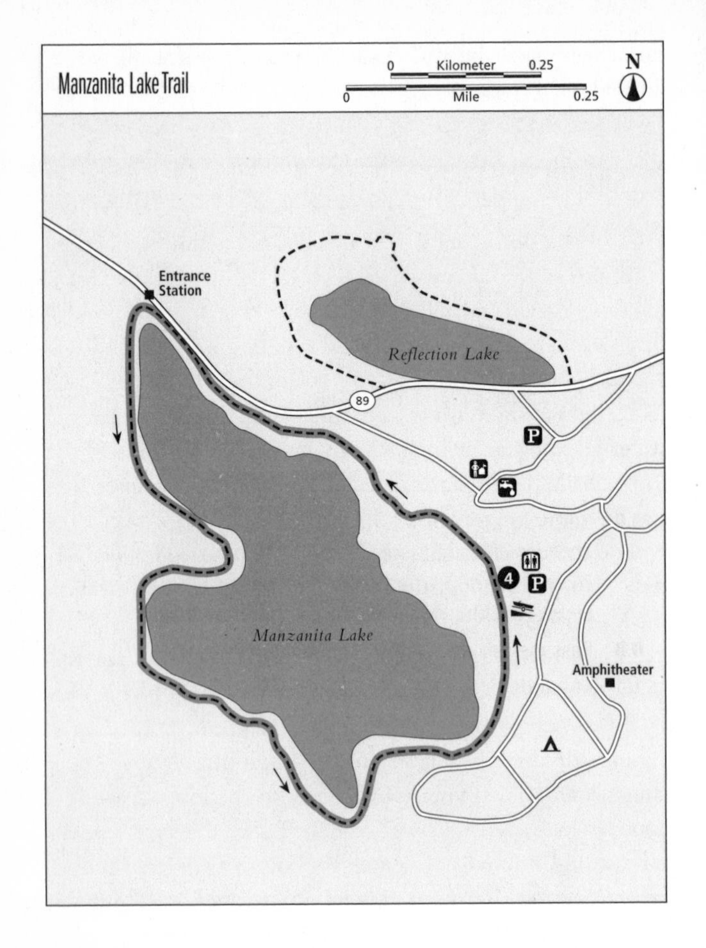

time), and it is easy to get lost in the beauty of this national park. The magic is enhanced during spring and fall butterfly migrations, when thousands of butterflies dance around hikers. Keep an eye out for the California tortoiseshell, often mistaken as a monarch. This similarly sized orange-and-black butterfly flourishes off manzanita bloom nectar, so it's no wonder such healthy mass-migrating populations flutter around Manzanita Lake.

If you'd like to see the lake at its finest, consider taking this hike around dawn. In the early morning it may only be you and the anglers soaking up the sunrise—all the more reason to stay at the wonderful campground. In the wee hours you might also hike with blue herons, geese, ducks, and other waterfowl taking advantage of these shores at the quieter times. Still feeling adventurous at the end of this 1.8-mile loop? Hop on the Manzanita Creek Trail, on the other side of the campground, for a change of scenery.

Miles and Directions

0.0 Beginning at the Manzanita Lake Trailhead, on the northern edge of the boat launch parking area, head west for a counterclockwise loop, following the trail as it detours along the creek to the Visitors Center.

0.8 Pass the second trailhead and Visitors Center.

1.8 Arrive back at the boat launch parking area.

5 Burney Falls Loop Trail

Edging the eastern bulge of the Cascade Range is this prize-worthy state park, home to the grandest of all waterfall hikes. Once deemed a wonder of the world by President Theodore Roosevelt, the positively picturesque Burney Falls humbles every visitor to set foot on its breezy loop trail. The short route is accessible year-round and swarms with visitors in the popular summer season. Whether the mecca is bustling with activity or abandoned in the icy wind, it is impossible not to be enchanted by the falls.

Distance: 1.2-mile loop
Approximate hiking time: 1 hour
Difficulty: Easy
Trail surface: Paved, rock, and dirt path
Best season: Year-round; prepare for snow and ice in winter
Other trail users: None
Canine compatibility: Dogs not permitted
Fees and permits: Day-use fee
Schedule: Day use only
Maps: TOPO! California CD, Disc 3; USGS Burney Falls, CA; California State Parks brochure: *McArthur-Burney Falls Memorial State Park*
Trail contacts: McArthur-Burney Falls Memorial State Park, 24898 CA 89, Burney, CA 96013; (530) 335-2777; www.parks.ca.gov

Finding the trailhead: From Redding take CA 299 about 54 miles east and turn north (left) onto CA 89. Drive 5.5 miles to the park entrance, then follow the road to the parking area on the left, just past the entrance station, at N41 00.802' / W121 39.034'.

The Hike

A hundred million gallons of water gush daily over the swift black flow known as Burney Falls. The undisputable pinup of area waterfalls never disappoints an onlooker, and the easy trail is suitable for everyone, adding to this hike's A-list status. With an excellent campground and spoiling amenities at the state park, this is a stroll worthy of a weekend and an overall excellent family outing.

The area's lineage stretches back to the 1860s, when the McArthur family helped to preserve the falls by purchasing surrounding land that would later be donated. Yet, no one knows too much about the region's namesake Samuel Burney, an incidental nineteenth-century drifter who died in a tiff with Native Americans and would somehow pass on his name to the area's highlights. The National Park Service declared this well-deserved waterfall a designated national landmark in 1984 and preserved the falls for all to enjoy. Later the area morphed into a state park complete with a campground, restaurant, picnic area, visitor center, and flush toilets. The Pacific Crest Trail even splices through the grounds, along with other tracks, inviting a secondary escapade.

The powerful waterfall is part of Burney Creek's flow, a feeder for the mighty Pit River. The 129-foot-tall falls plunge over deep gray basaltic columns and crash forcefully into a stunning aquamarine pool. The chilly water remains a crisp 42–48°F, and the cloudy mist produces an absolutely indulgent 65°F breeze on those cooking Cascadian days. Be cautious on this cooled clip of the trail; the path can get slippery around the poolside boulders. Most visitors to Burney

Falls rush down to the base of the falls for the trophy photo, then head straight back up, depriving themselves of the full loop, which is a shame since this hike comes full circle through the amazing habitat.

Allow for ample time at the base of the waterfall to absorb the sight, sound, and touch of the misty giant. Once you're ready to press on, follow the trail opposite the way you came, as it slinks around a corner between the creek and a mossy talus slope. As you move farther away from the falls, you'll notice a quick shift back to the season's climate as well as a change from the hardwood forest. Ponderosa pine and Douglas fir mesh into black oak, vine maple, dogwood, willow, and alder.

A small footbridge hops over Burney Creek and leads to the hillside climb. The elevation is dispersed over a long switchback. If you pause to catch your breath on one of the benches, look below for anglers wading the creek in search of trout. The top of the hill overlooks the start of the falls, lending a nice perspective of the seemingly calm creek above. If you followed this interesting little watershed upriver, it would soon seem to disappear underground, then miraculously reappear sometime later. There, the flow travels underground in the porous depths of the lava beds that funnel it to the falls.

After moving on from the creek to the top overlook, the route levels out and drifts through white and black oak groves, manzanita clusters, flowering currants, and even a few frolicking frogs before it crosses a second footbridge to reach the main road. A brief leg of the trail ribbons the road before the route concludes at the trailhead.

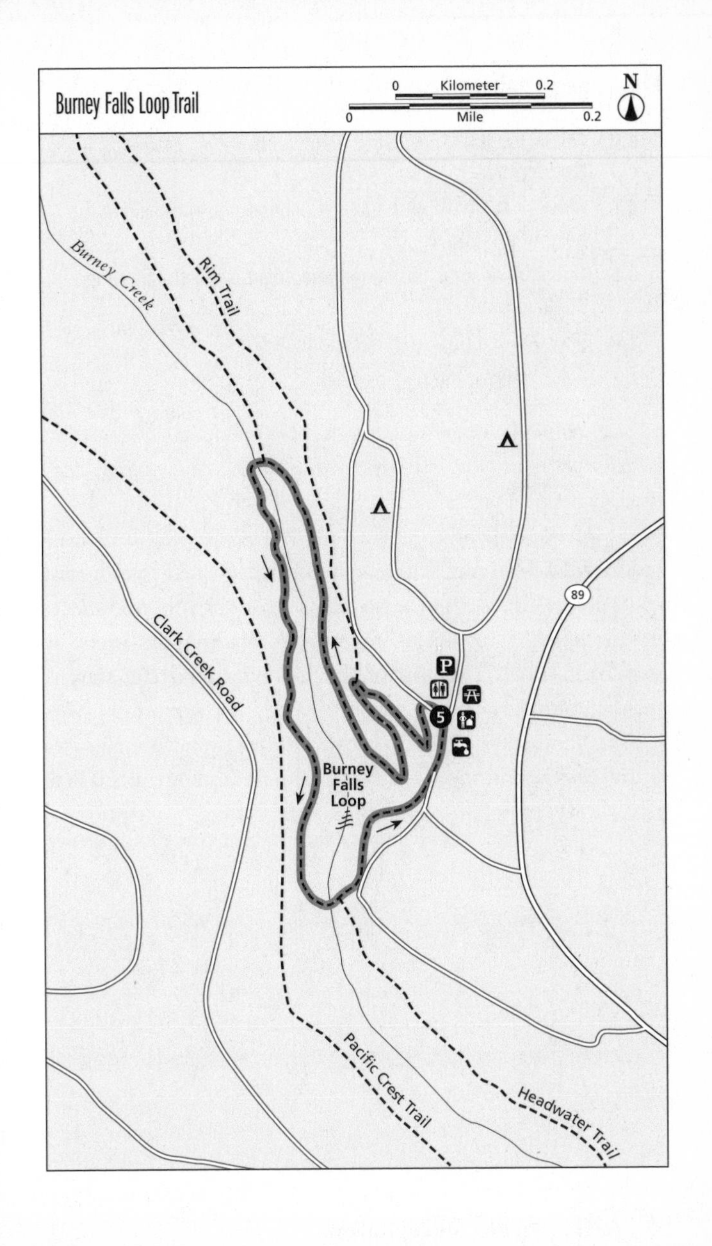

Burney Falls Loop Trail
0
Kilometer
0.2
0
Mile
0.2
N
Burney Creek
Rim Trail
89
Clark Creek Road
5
Burney
Falls
Loop
Pacific Crest Trail
Headwater Trail

Miles and Directions

0.0 Follow the trail 150 feet to reach an overlook. Stay right for the loop trail.

0.3 Arrive at the base of the falls. Continue northwest along the base of the falls.

0.5 Go left over small footbridge, then right and left, following the loop trail.

1.0 Stay left and pass over second footbridge.

1.2 Arrive back at the parking area.

6 McCloud River Falls

In less than 2 miles, three glorious waterfalls dot this easy hike near McCloud. Each cascade has a unique flavor—one a stout flow into a popular swimming hole, another a wide-mouth guzzle into a frothy pool, and the last a roaring rapid piercing a narrow gorge. En route to the falls, soak up the recreational delights, including swimming, fishing, and picnicking.

Distance: 3.6-mile out-and-back
Approximate hiking time: 2 hours
Difficulty: Easy
Trail surface: Dirt path
Best season: Spring through fall
Other trail users: Mountain bikers, equestrians
Canine compatibility: Leashed dogs permitted
Fees and permits: None
Schedule: Day use only; facilities not maintained in winter, with possible road closures in the snowy months
Maps: TOPO! California CD, Disc 3; USGS Lake McCloud, CA
Trail contacts: Shasta-Trinity National Forest, McCloud Ranger Station, P.O. Box 1620, 2019 Forest Rd., McCloud, CA 96057; (530) 964-2184; www.fs.fed.us/r5/shastatrinity

Finding the trailhead: From Redding take I-5 north for about 55 miles and take exit 736, CA 89, to McCloud. Drive 15 miles (5 miles east of McCloud) and turn south onto the unsigned forest road (FR 40N44) at the sign for Fowlers Campground and Lower Falls. Drive 0.6 mile and turn right at the sign for Lower Falls. After another 0.6 mile, turn left into the Shasta-Trinity National Forest Lower Falls Picnic Area at N41 14.418' / W122 01.495'. Park here and pick up the trail at the overlook.

The Hike

The full fury of the McCloud River stretches about 50 miles, from its sopping birth in the Cascades a few miles shy of Mount Shasta to several drainages, including the Pit River. Much like connect the dots, this relaxed trail links a few of the river's waterfalls through a thick forest and impressive canyon. The 1.8-mile one-way stretch may be the most scenic slice of the McCloud River.

You can hop on the trail at a couple of different locations, including a parking area at each of the three falls. Lower Falls, the most humble of the tumbles, is a nice place to start the day, as many do. Here you will find popular picnicking grounds, restrooms, and water. From the parking lot it is just a couple hundred feet to the falls overlook and trail. After you've absorbed the information at the interpretive sign, walk down the stairs to the base of the squat falls.

If you have time, lounge around on one of the poolside boulders or take a quick dip in the wonderful swimming hole at the base of Lower Falls. When your time is up, follow the paved trail to the left of the pool upstream. The course quickly turns to dirt and zigzags through Fowlers Campground. Once all the activity of Lower Falls and the campground fades behind you, the canyon narrows. Look out for bald eagles perched atop the towering pines, cedars, and firs.

The hike continues along the crystal-clear river for the next 0.5 mile until it reaches the second waterfall. At Middle Falls the river seems to be sliced in two and terraced where the 100-foot-wide mouth drops 50 feet into a swirling pool. Several large shaded boulders beckon for a break. After you've paid homage to the prettiest falls of the trio, head back on track, climbing extra-long switchbacks to a lofty overlook above Middle Falls, where you will also find another well-developed parking and picnic area.

Once again, the course snakes through the overlook before spitting you out on a ridge. Here the canyon is predominantly below you, and the narrow trail hangs over a steep drop to the river on the right (exercise caution with the young ones). The hike slopes subtly down the last 0.5 mile to the final waterfall. At Upper Falls, the swiftest of the lot, you'll find a slim flow bursting through a narrow gorge with the full force of the condensed river feeding it. Steel fencing encourages you to stay on the trail above the falls, but many people follow social trails down to the base. The tricky footing is for confident trailblazers only. Although the recommended stopping point is this lookout, the main trail continues on for another several miles into the backcountry and the Algoma Campground.

Backtracking to the Lower Falls trailhead offers the best mountain vistas, and you often run into photographers on the trail. In the winter months the rimside trail perfectly frames snowcapped Mount Shasta with ponderosa pines. Now that the anticipation of the falls has been fulfilled, keep an eye peeled for chipmunks and squirrels, ospreys, many songbirds, and an occasional black-belted kingfisher or willow flycatcher. You might also catch an angler throwing a line into one of the most bountiful trout rivers in the region.

Miles and Directions

0.0 Begin the trail at the Lower Falls Overlook, following the paved river trail. After a couple hundred yards, the pavement will end.

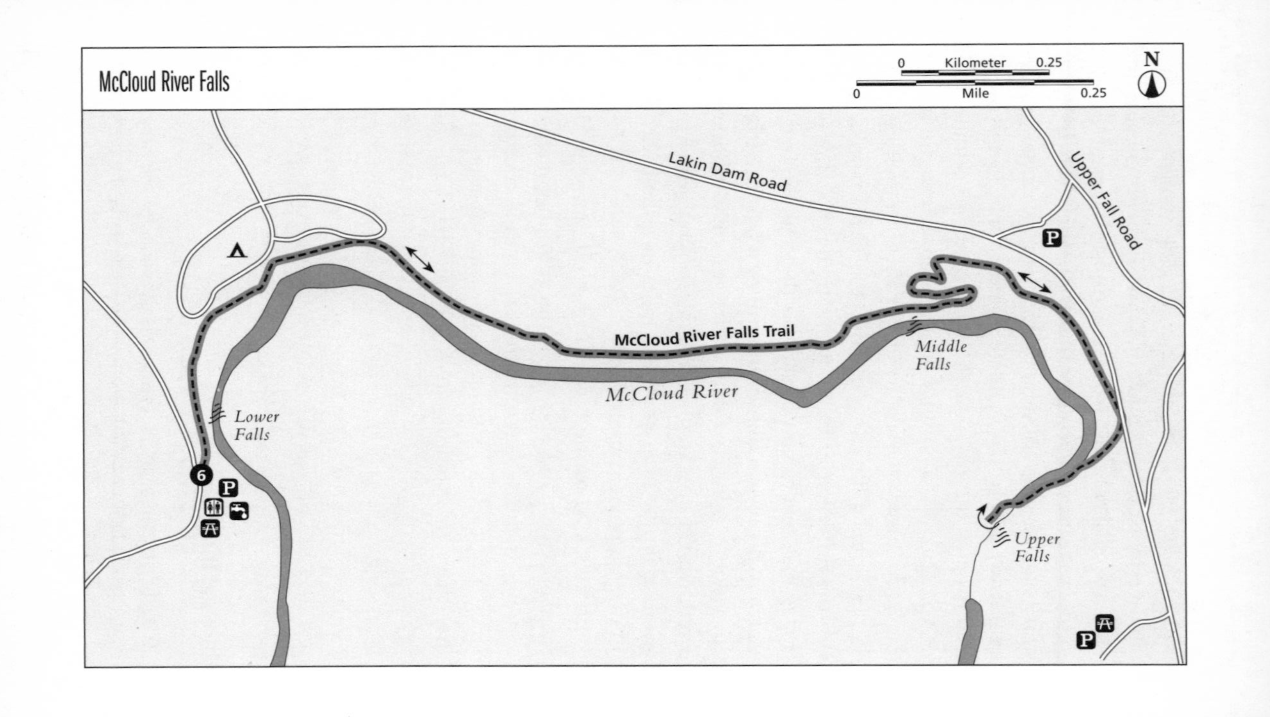
McCloud River Falls
0
Kilometer
0.25
0
Mile
0.25
N
Lakin Dam Road
Upper Fall Road
McCloud River Falls Trail
McCloud River
Lower Falls
Middle Falls
Upper Falls
6

0.3 Stay right as the trail winds through Fowlers Campground.

0.5 Follow the trail sign to the right for Middle Falls.

1.2 Reach Middle Falls.

1.4 Stay right as you cross through the Middle Falls Overlook.

1.8 Reach the Upper Falls Overlook, backtrack from here.

3.6 Arrive back at the Lower Falls Overlook.

7 Squaw Valley Creek Trail

This lush waterfront route not far from McCloud blooms in tiger lilies and soaks in chilled shade. Cooled by a couple of rapids and rich foliage, this aquatic gem is a good choice for a summer hike. The moderate 6-mile one-way Squaw Valley Creek Trail can be lengthened or shortened, or combined with the intersecting Pacific Crest Trail.

Distance: 12-mile out-and-back or 8.5-mile loop
Approximate hiking time: 4–5 hours
Difficulty: Moderate
Trail surface: Dirt and rock path
Best season: Spring through fall
Other trail users: Mountain bikers, equestrians
Canine compatibility: Leashed dogs permitted
Fees and permits: None
Schedule: None; hike only accessible in the snow-free months, approximately Apr through Nov
Maps: TOPO! California CD, Disc 3; USGS Girard Ridge, CA
Trail contacts: Shasta-Trinity National Forest, McCloud Ranger Station, P.O. Box 1620, 2019 Forest Rd., McCloud, CA 96057; (530) 964-2184; www.fs.fed.us/r5/shastatrinity
Special considerations: New restroom

Finding the trailhead: From Redding take I-5 north for about 55 miles and take exit 736 east onto CA 89 toward McCloud. Drive 9.5 miles on CA 89 to McCloud and turn right onto Squaw Valley Creek Road (NF11) at the sign for the McCloud Reservoir. Drive for 6.2 miles and turn right onto the unlabeled gravel road at the sign for Squaw Valley Creek. Drive 3 miles to the Cabin Creek Trailhead on the left at N41 08.611' / W122 10.189'.

The Hike

The Squaw Valley Creek Trail was still being developed in 2009, and although it lacked a proper trailhead, a modern vault toilet and small parking area mark the beginning of the route. Don't let the primitive parking area dissuade you from this hike that stretches 5 cool, crisp miles one-way from Squaw Valley Creek Road to Bear Trap Creek. The invigorating route is well labeled once you begin, and passes a series of miniature waterfalls and speedy rapids. This is a gentle choice for backpackers and has plenty of places to fish, swim, and camp, so it is no wonder you commonly run into people heading out for a weekend.

For a brief moment when you begin this trail, you will also be walking on the Pacific Crest Trail (PCT), the infamous footway that leads hearty hikers from Mexico to Canada. Shortly, however, Squaw Valley Creek Trail heads off on its own, and the junction for the PCT splits near a footbridge. The independent Squaw Valley Creek Trail perpetually hugs the western lip of the creek through a mixed deciduous evergreen forest of mature pine, cedar, fir, Pacific yew, and oak.

The verdant creek side looks as if it has been plucked from the tropics, with a healthy layer of deep green shrubs. One particular prehistoric-looking plant stands out among others: Indian rhubarb, also known as the umbrella plant, grows in healthy bushels along the creek. It's identifiable by its giant, waxy green leaves, which grow up to 2 feet long. The plants unique stems stretch up several feet and blossom with a cluster of pink flowers in spring. Indian rhubarb is known for its medicinal uses, but the leaves are poisonous and the stems must be properly cooked, so don't sample this curiosity on the trail.

From spring through late summer, other wild blooms break up the rich greens of the riparian zone. The drooping bells of pink Pacific bleeding heart, light purple wild ginger, yellow violet, and wild rose also show their colors. Along the mossy rock walls to your right, distinct cliff maids cling to the rocks, their light pink and white petals unique to the region. In fall, vine maple, oak, and the abundant poison oak change into their brilliantly colored shields. A series of whipping rapids and waterfalls occurs around the 2- and 3-mile mark, with social trails leading to the falls and small swimming holes. The stout surges are all under 10 feet tall but handsome nevertheless, energizing the trail just as you feel you've grown accustomed to the scenery.

Half of the expedition ends when you reach Bear Trap Creek and an old road. On the return, study the wealth of wildlife you may have overlooked. Stop on one of the many basaltic boulders by the creek and listen for songbirds. You might also notice the flickering dance of a petite dark gray bird along the shore. This water-diving bird may seem plain upon first glance, but the American dipper, also known as the water ouzel, was noted by John Muir as his favorite bird.

Miles and Directions

0.0 Begin at the unlabeled Cabin Creek Trailhead and head south onto the unlabeled Squaw Valley Creek Trail, crossing a small footbridge after 200 feet.

0.2 At the intersection with the second footbridge, stay right, following the signs for the PCT/Squaw Valley Creek Trail.

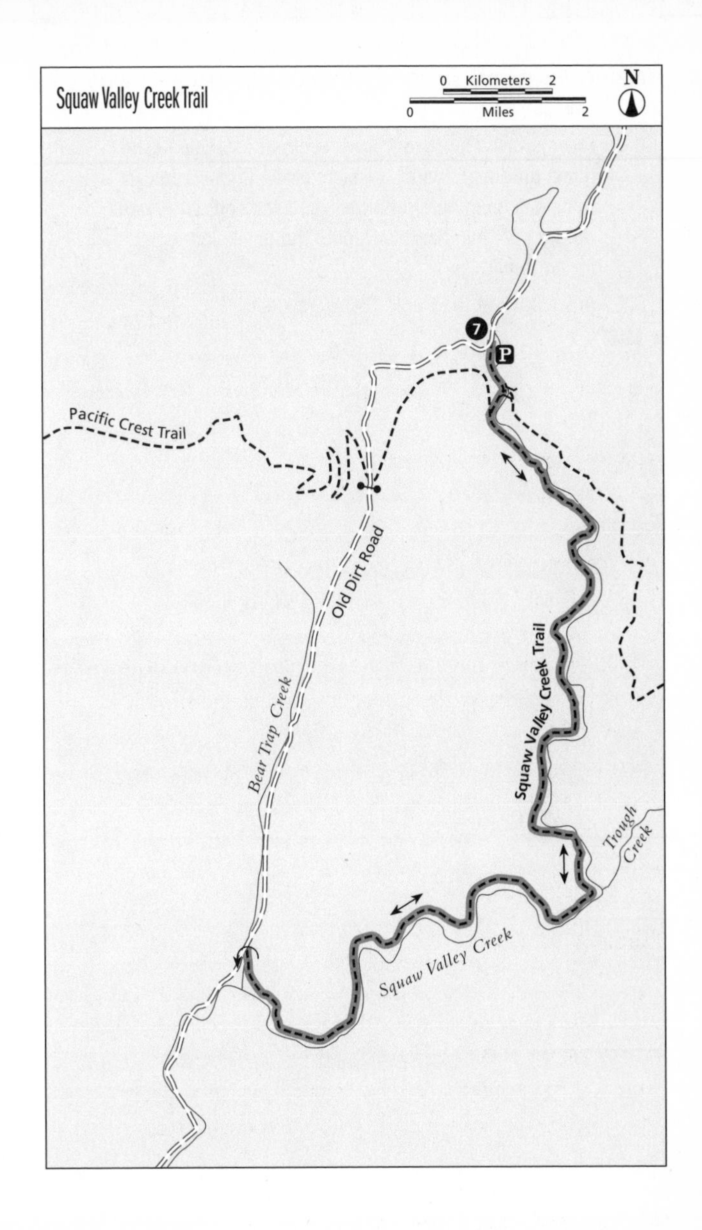
Squaw Valley Creek Trail
0 Kilometers 2
0 Miles 2
N
7
P
Pacific Crest Trail
Old Dirt Road
Bear Trap Creek
Squaw Valley Creek Trail
Trough Creek
Squaw Valley Creek

0.3 Follow the trail straight, continuing south, as the PCT forks right.

6.0 Cross a rustic footbridge and reach an unlabeled gravel forest road and end at the sign for the Cabin Creek Trail. Backtrack from here for an easy 12-mile out-and-back hike, or turn right, heading north onto the unlabeled forest road, for an 8-mile loop.

8.5 or 12.0 Arrive back at the Cabin Creek Trailhead.

8 Bunny Flat to Horse Camp

If you're not ready to climb to the top of Mount Shasta, the day hike from Bunny Flat to Horse Camp is the next best thing. This high-altitude trail treks nearly 2 miles up the south flank of the mountain. It is a moderately challenging route but offers a taste of Mount Shasta's world-renowned mountaineering flavor. It is also the first steps of the most popular route to the 14,162-foot summit.

Distance: 3.4-mile out-and-back
Approximate hiking time: 4 hours (allow time to explore Horse Camp)
Difficulty: More challenging (due to high altitude)
Trail surface: Dirt and rock path
Best season: Summer
Other trail users: None
Canine compatibility: Dogs not permitted at Horse Camp
Fees and permits: A wilderness permit, available at the trailhead or ranger station, is required to access this trail. There is a day-use fee in summer, and the permit is free in winter (although a donation for day use is suggested).
Schedule: Trail open year-round but only accessible to hikers without snow equipment from summer though early fall, approximately June through Sept
Maps: TOPO! California CD, Disc 3; Shasta-Trinity National Forest leaflet: *Squaw Valley Creek Trail;* USGS Girard Ridge and Yellow-jacket Mountain, CA; USFS
Trail contacts: Shasta-Trinity National Forest, Mount Shasta Ranger Station, 204 West Alma, Mount Shasta, CA 96067; (530) 926-4511; www.fs.fed.us/r5/shastatrinity
Special considerations: Always call ahead to the ranger station to check trail conditions if you choose this route in spring or fall. There is no water at this trailhead. This is a high-altitude hike. Most people aren't heavily affected by the altitude, but the thin air should be taken into account.

Finding the trailhead: As you drive I-5 north of Redding, Mount Shasta seems to be placed smack dab in the middle of the freeway. From Redding head north on I-5 about 58 miles and take the Central Mount Shasta exit (number 738) west. Turn right (east) onto West Lake Street. Drive 0.8 mile and follow the road as it turns into the Everett Memorial Highway. Follow the highway 11.1 miles to the Bunny Flat Trailhead on your left at N41 21.256' / W122 13.962'.

The Hike

You can't help but wonder what it is like to climb Mount Shasta. Lonesome and dominant, the behemoth beauty tauntingly appears in nearly every northern vista of the Redding region. Amplifying the dramatic sight, the mountain seems to come out of nowhere, overshadowing the encompassing valley below.

Mount Shasta is California's fifth-largest peak and the second-highest mountain of the Cascade Range. The Cascades are a string of volcanic mountains pushed up by the force of an oceanic plate subducted by California's continental plate. This range is just a segment of the Pacific Ring of Fire, a more extensive series of volcanoes built in similar episodes. One glance at Shasta, and it is no surprise you're looking at a volcano. The steep-sided conical mountain was created by multiple layers of volcanic ash and mudflows. The volcano slumbers these days, without an eruption since 1786—and none predicted to come soon.

If you're not up to the strenuous eleven-hour or two-day journey to the summit of Mount Shasta, consider the hike from Bunny Flat to Horse Camp. Here you get the chance to walk the first couple miles of the most popular trail to the top, known as Avalanche Gulch or the John

Muir Route. With plenty of mountaineers gearing up for their climb, even the trailhead is exciting!

Bunny Flat Trailhead is located at a whopping 7,000-foot elevation, and a hike to Horse Camp will climb an additional 1,000 feet. The route is fairly exposed, gliding through a small meadow of low-lying grass and mixed fir forest with striking eye-stretching vistas. Around a mile in, the trail from Sand Flat will merge from the left and join the climb up (or down) the mountain. Horse Camp is located 1.75 miles up the trail at just about the time things start to get really rocky. The area around Horse Camp is private property belonging to the Sierra Club and is managed cooperatively with the national forest. Here you will see an old 1920s cabin made of volcanic rock and red fir, which houses a petite visitor center and library. Horse Camp also has low-impact campsites, composting toilets, and a seasonal source of water from a spring nearby. If you decide to extend your hike up the jagged slope of the Olberman's Causeway, be sure to consult one of the volunteers at Horse Camp for more information.

This trail is buried in snow through the winter, and the white coat can linger through summer. Several glaciers still dot Mount Shasta's top. Dress in layers accordingly and always check the status of this trail. If you do visit in spring or early summer, the snow-covered mountain is a beautiful sight. Upon his visit to the area, President Theodore Roosevelt said he considered the evening twilight on Mount Shasta one of the grandest sights he had ever witnessed—surely a reference to the pastel hues that beam off the mountain's soft curves in those magical hours.

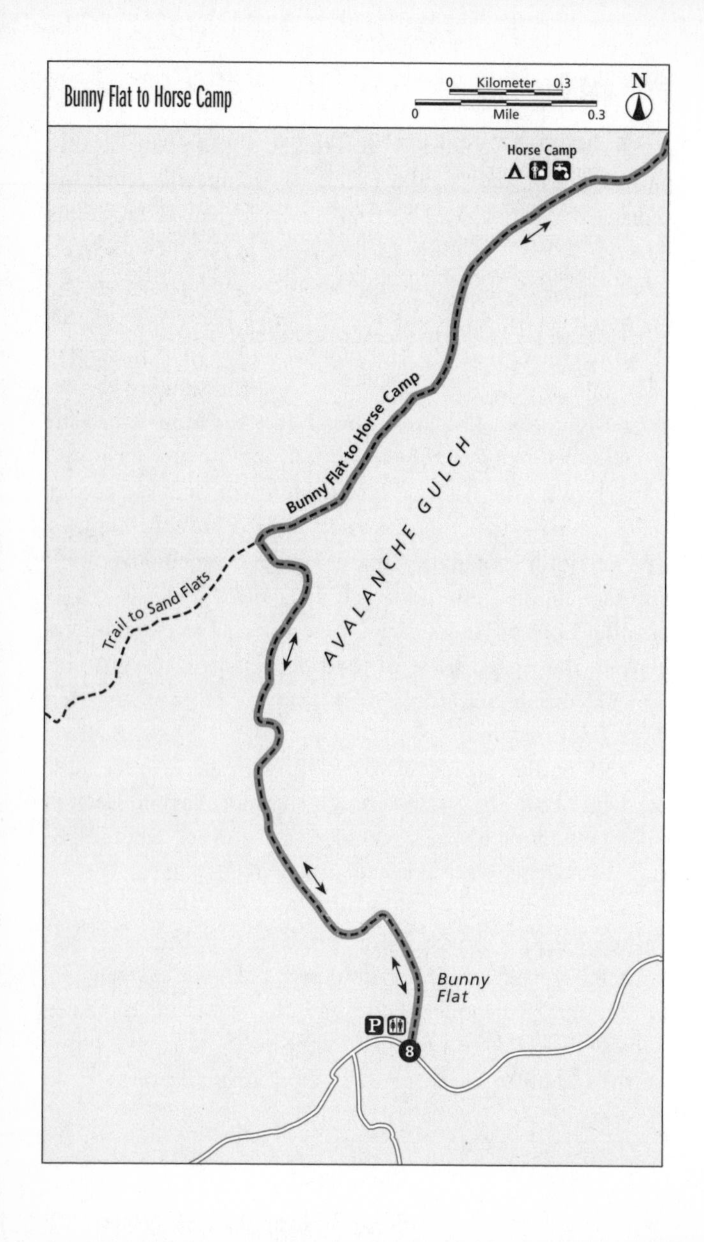
Bunny Flat to Horse Camp
0 Kilometer 0.3
0 Mile 0.3
N
Horse Camp
Bunny Flat to Horse Camp
AVALANCHE GULCH
Trail to Sand Flats
Bunny
Flat
P
8

Miles and Directions

0.0 Beginning at the Bunny Flat Trailhead, stay right as other trails intersect with the trail to Horse Camp.

1.2 Look for an easy-to-miss sign posted about 10 feet up on a tree trunk labeled "No Dogs." This is where the route ends for those traveling with canines. Other hikers should continue north to Horse Camp.

1.7 Arrive at Horse Camp, backtrack from here or continue on Avalanche Gulch for an extension (inquire at the cabin for more information).

3.4 Arrive back at the Bunny Flat Trailhead.

9 Castle Lake Trail

On a sunny day when the gleaming glacial-melt waters of Castle Lake lie still under the backdrop of Mount Shasta, the views from this short trail are worth a hundred-mile hike. Not far from Mount Shasta City, the Klamath Mountain stroll offers plenty of options, from a 1-mile out-and-back along the lake's western shore to a backpacking trip down to Castle Crags.

Distance: 1-mile out-and-back (with longer options)
Approximate hiking time: 30 minutes
Difficulty: Moderate
Trail surface: Dirt and rock path
Best season: Late spring through fall
Other trail users: Mountain bikers
Canine compatibility: Leashed dogs permitted
Fees and permits: None
Schedule: None
Maps: TOPO! California CD, Disc 2; USGS Seven Lakes Basin and Dunsmuir, CA; USFS Castle Crags Wilderness
Trail contacts: Shasta-Trinity National Forest, Mount Shasta Ranger Station, 204 West Alma, Mount Shasta, CA 96067; (530) 926-4511; www.fs.fed.us/r5/shastatrinity
Special considerations: No facilities at the trailhead

Finding the trailhead: From Redding take I-5 north about 58 miles and take the Central Mount Shasta exit (number 738) west. Make a quick left onto South Old Stage Road and right onto W. A. Barr Road. Drive 2.2 miles, crossing the dam over Lake Siskiyou, and turn left onto Castle Lake Road. Travel 7 miles to the trailhead at N41 13.877' / W122 22.959'.

The Hike

The beautiful aquamarine tint of Castle Lake displays something about its geologic history. Castle Lake is a cirque lake, carved and filled by a glacier over 10,000 years ago. *Cirque* is a geologic term based on a French word for semicircle and refers to the rock wall that wedges in one side of the lake. Along the steep, glacially carved wall the lake is about 100 feet deep, whereas closer to earthen shores it's only about 15 feet deep. Castle Lake itself is rather small, around fifty acres in size, but nonetheless large in year-round charm.

Pick up the Castle Lake Trail west from the parking area, avoiding the eastern route. Follow the rocky, but easy, hike along the western lip of the lake through a thick, healthy overstory forest of pine, alder, fir, and cedar, and an understory of oak, wispy vine maple, and dogwood. The area is also packed with plant and animal species. You might spy river otter, garter snake, cascade frog, or someone fishing for trout. Black bear and deer also visit the grounds. Both bald and golden eagles are a common sight overhead.

This incredibly rich ecosystem creates the perfect host for the on-site research station, the Castle Lake Limnological Research Station, a partnered education center and living lab for University of California–Davis and University of Nevada–Reno. Limnology is the scientific study of fresh water, and this sensitive ecosystem is the perfect host. Recorded studies of the lake date back to 1959. Although you can't visit the research station, the wildlife is easy to spot.

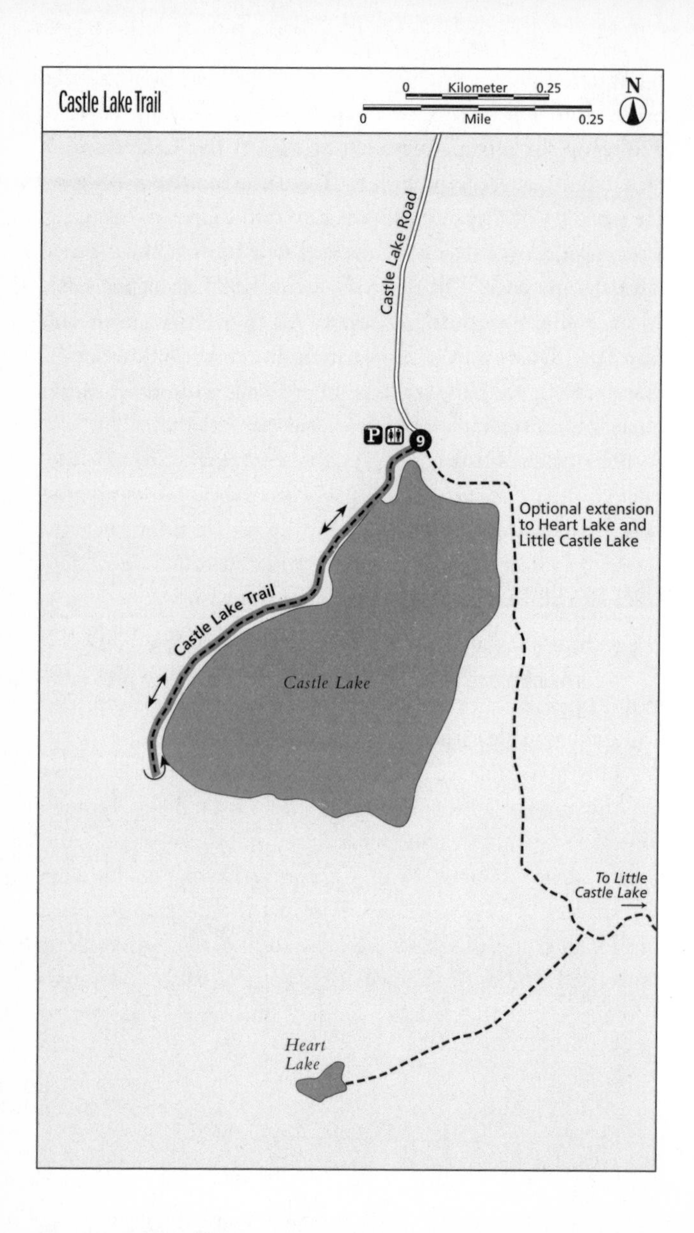
Castle Lake Trail
0
Kilometer
0.25
0
Mile
0.25
N
Castle Lake Road
P
9
Optional extension
to Heart Lake and
Little Castle Lake
Castle Lake Trail
Castle Lake
To Little
Castle Lake
Heart
Lake

When you've reached the dead-end at the 0.5-mile mark, you will have to backtrack to the parking area. If you're up for more adventure, return to the trailhead and pick up the route heading east from the southern edge of the parking lot. From here you can hike to Heart Lake and Little Castle Lake (follow the social spur trails to the right at the 0.5-mile and 2-mile marks) for a highly recommended 1- or 2-mile roundtrip extension. Look for lilies along the lake and unique purple Shasta penstemon in the grasslands. Also making an appearance is the wild-looking red columbine flower, which looks like an orange octopus blooming atop a slender stem. If you continue on this trail, you can hike clear up Mount Bradley. Consult the local ranger station for maps and information.

Miles and Directions

0.0 From the northeast corner of the parking area, pick up the unlabeled trail behind the restrooms and head west onto the dirt path.

0.5 The trail dead-ends, backtrack from here.

1.0 Arrive back at the parking area.

10 Castle Crags State Park: Indian Creek Nature Trail

Castle Crags State Park's Indian Creek Nature Trail is an interesting little loop full of information on the history and life of the region. The easy 1-mile trail travels though a thick forest along the shallow creek. You can also tack on the intersecting Flume Trail, which follows a historical water route. Or better yet, bring your tent and spend a weekend camped out at the beautiful campground and explore the 30-plus miles of trail within the park.

Distance: 1-mile lollipop (with longer options)
Approximate hiking time: 30 minutes
Difficulty: Easy
Trail surface: Dirt and rock path
Best season: Year-round
Other trail users: None
Canine compatibility: Dogs not permitted
Fees and permits: Day-use fee
Schedule: Day use only
Maps: TOPO! California CD, Discs 2 and 3; USGS Dunsmuir, CA; USFS Castle Crags Wilderness
Trail contacts: Castle Crags State Park, P.O. Box 80, Castella, CA 96017; (530) 235-2684; www.parks.ca.gov
Special considerations: There may be snow on this trail during the winter months

Finding the trailhead: You will notice the mountain-high crags long before you reach the Castella exit on I-5 north of Redding. They are a superb sight to behold; everyone look (but the driver)! From Redding take I-5 north about 45 miles to exit 724 (Castella) and turn west (left) onto Castle Creek Road. Drive 0.3 mile and turn right into Castle Crags State Park. The trail is on your left at the small circular parking area adjacent to the fee station at N41 08.870' /

W122 19.298'. Be sure to pick up your interpretive guide at the fee station.

The Hike

Castle Crags State Park's "crags" refer to eroding granitic remains of a massive pluton that is more than 200 million years old. A pluton is a chamber of cooled magma that crystallized into igneous rocks miles beneath the Earth's surface. Over time the processes of erosion have sculpted the mighty dome into scraggly exposed pinnacles. The sparkling gray formations bust out of the mountain peaks at an elevation of over 6,000 feet, creating a dramatic display. One unique outcrop, Castle Dome, has been likened to Yosemite's Half Dome.

Castle Crags State Park was established to protect the area, and the watershed, from the mining boom and railroad development of the 1850s. Successfully preserved by concerned citizens almost a century ago, the first pieces of the park were made official by the early 1930s. Today, the forested playground is over 10,000 acres in size and home to a beautiful and well-developed campground and numerous hiking trails. The easy River Trail crosses a daring suspension footbridge over the Sacramento River, the strenuous Crags Trail climbs to Castle Dome, and even the Pacific Crest Trail snakes through the grounds.

At the heart of the park, the Indian Creek Nature Trail is a quick but rewarding jaunt, offering a crash course on native flora, fauna, and human history. The wide, well-manicured trail travels along dirt and pine-needle footing through large fir, pine, mature incense cedar, and scraggly white and black oak. Blackbirds, bluebirds, jays, and robins swoop through the canopy. Delightful smells of pine and sounds of the creek accompany the saunter.

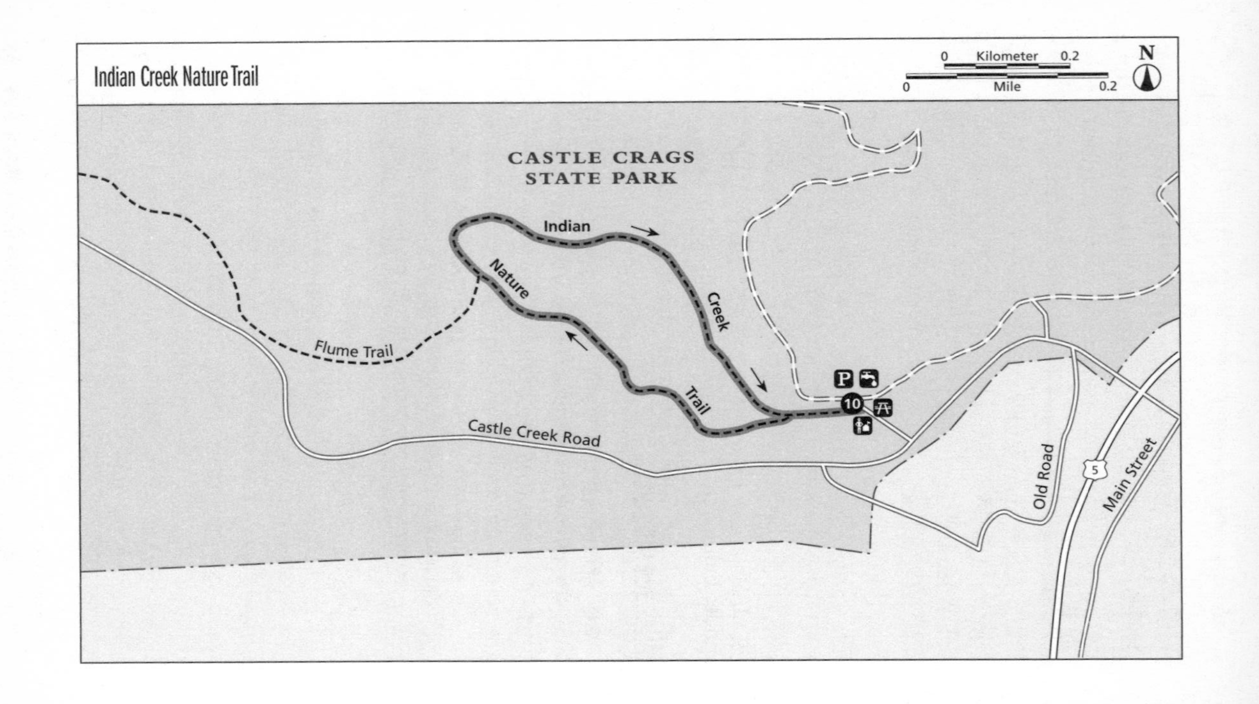
Indian Creek Nature Trail
0
Kilometer
0.2
0
Mile
0.2
N
CASTLE CRAGS
STATE PARK
Indian
Creek
Nature
Trail
Flume Trail
Castle Creek Road
10
Old Road
5
Main Street

From the parking area it is only a few hundred feet to the loop section of the trail. Head left for a clockwise hike to correspond with the interpretive guide's numbered posts. Two cute stone bridges cross the creek, and the crags come into view over the treetops. Around the 0.5-mile mark, Flume Trail forks left. This is an interesting out-and-back extension along an old water ditch that once supplied the town of Castella. Back on the trail, the loop continues as it climbs a slow 150-foot grade up a hill, then slopes down on the return. Indian Creek Nature Trail is an overall nice choice for a summer hike, when the shady evergreen canopy offers a year-round shield. The trail was scheduled for an update in summer 2010, with new posts and interpretive guide; inquire at the entrance station.

Miles and Directions

0.0 After picking up a copy of the interpretive guide at the trailhead, walk 500 feet to reach the intersection of the loop.

0.5 The intersection with the Flume Trail is to the left; stay right to continue on the Indian Creek Nature Trail. For a longer option, go left on the Flume Trail, which will tack on an additional 1.5 miles round-trip for an out-and-back to the environmental campsites (although the Flume continues from there).

1.0 Arrive back at the trailhead.

11 Pacific Crest Trail to Burstarse Falls

This snippet of the mighty Pacific Crest Trail (PCT) is a few miles west of Castle Crags State Park. The portion to Burstarse Falls leads through a stunning section of the Trinity Mountains with sweeping views and a seasonal waterfall. Although it is a cardio challenge to reach the PCT portion, once there, the rolling mountainside hike doesn't disappoint.

Distance: 4.8-mile out-and-back (with longer options)
Approximate hiking time: 3 hours
Difficulty: Moderate (with a 0.7-mile more-challenging ascent)
Trail surface: Rock and dirt path
Best season: Spring through fall (this hike may be inaccessible in winter due to snow)
Other trail users: Mountain bikers, equestrians
Canine compatibility: Leashed dogs permitted
Fees and permits: None
Schedule: None
Maps: TOPO! California CD, Discs 2 and 3; USGS Dunsmuir; USFS Castle Crags Wilderness
Trail contacts: Shasta-Trinity National Forest, Mount Shasta Ranger Station, 204 West Alma, Mount Shasta, CA 96067, (530) 926-4511, www.fs.fed.us/r5/shastatrinity; Pacific Crest Trail Association, (916) 349-2109 (office), (888) PC-TRAIL (728-7245) (trail conditions), www.pcta.org
Special considerations: There are no facilities at this trailhead; stop by Castle Crags State Park to top off the water bottle and take advantage of day-use facilities (small day-use fee). Dogs are allowed on this portion of the Pacific Crest Trail, but not on other portions. To find out more about extending your hike on the Pacific Crest Trail, contact the Pacific Crest Trail Association.

Finding the trailhead: From Redding take I-5 north for about 45 miles to exit 724 (Castella) and head west (left) onto Castle Creek Road. Drive 3.3 miles down the paved road and turn right into the small gravel-pit parking area, near a rustic sign labeled PCT, at N41 09.731' / W122 22.149'.

The Hike

Etched in the landscape from the deserts of Mexico to the Cascadian peaks of Canada, the Pacific Crest Trail (PCT) is arguably the most famous footpath in California. This legendary masterpiece is coveted by hikers and backpackers as one of the greatest trails in the United States and is designated an America's National Scenic Trail. You don't have to be a hard-core hiker to enjoy the route, however. In the Redding region alone, there are a dozen or so excellent access points to jump on and off the trail. The locale along Castle Creek Road offers a fine day hike and a good taste of the PCT, but your limbs will have to pay the price of a sharp ascent to reach the ridgeline system.

Fortunately, the 800-foot grade is distributed over several switchbacks and 0.75 mile of trail, but the uneven rock footing is still demanding. On the bright side, the views are almost immediately rewarding, so allow plenty of time to lug up the dry jagged hillside. If you pause to soak in the Castle Creek Valley below, the grade won't seem so laborious.

The trail begins in the northwestern corner of the parking area, which is little more than an old gravel pit. The trail appears to have once been labeled and is commonly known as Dog Trail. Follow the rocky switchbacks uphill aside immense incense cedar, Douglas fir, towering pine, and creeping false azalea. The Dog Trail portion dead-ends at the PCT, where you can head left for the journey to Burstarse Falls. If you go right, heading south along the PCT, several rolling miles bring you to Castle Crags State Park and, if you keep going, Mexico.

Heading west along the PCT, the high-rise trail rolls over gentle drops and gains. Western backdrops of breath-taking Castle Crags sprawl between patches of black oak and mixed conifer forest. This is a nice hike to pack along the camera. Not much is labeled on the trail, but you will pass seasonal Popcorn Spring, which has a sign. When you reach Burstarse Creek, follow it upstream along the rocky edges, carefully watching your footing on the slippery boulders. A little effort produces the cool reward of a 40-foot waterfall (or the big shaded boulders that remain where the plum-meting cascade once flowed, depending on the season).

This waterfall dries up by midsummer, but the loss of liquid doesn't lessen the scenery of the trail—especially in fall, when maples and oaks show their colors. Watch out for one such beautiful, but noxious, plant: Disguised as a young oak, poison oak will wreak havoc on the skin of its victims. One quick swipe onto clothing or skin leaves behind an oil that infectiously spreads an irritating rash. This plant can be identified by its distinctive three-clustered leaves. When in doubt, memorize the saying, "Leaves of three, let it be!" Bugs can also get nasty on this trail and seem to endure through the bitterly cold months, so don't forget the bug spray.

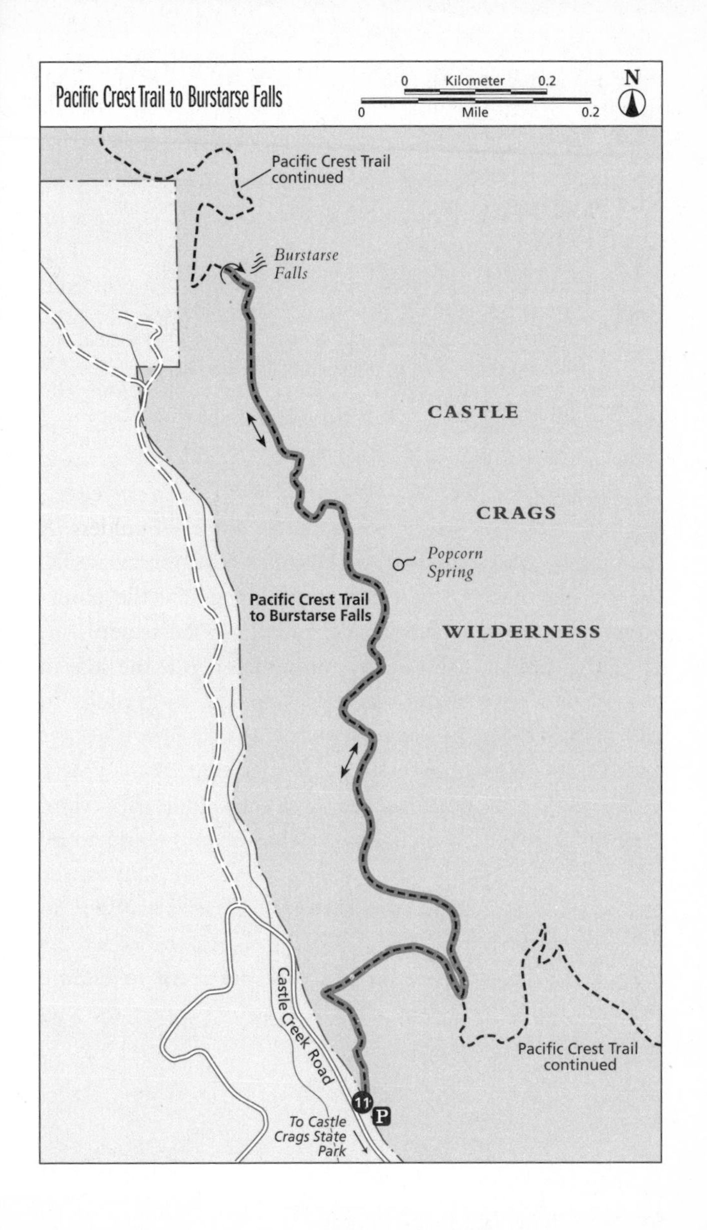
Pacific Crest Trail to Burstarse Falls
0 Kilometer 0.2
0 Mile 0.2
N
Pacific Crest Trail continued
Burstarse Falls
CASTLE
CRAGS
WILDERNESS
Popcorn Spring
Pacific Crest Trail to Burstarse Falls
Castle Creek Road
Pacific Crest Trail continued
11
P
To Castle Crags State Park

Miles and Directions

0.0 Beginning at the northwestern corner of the parking area, follow the rustic PCT sign.

0.7 Dead-end into the Pacific Crest Trail (PCT). Turn left for Burstarse Falls.

1.7 Pass Popcorn Spring (which is dry by midsummer).

2.4 Arrive at Burstarse Creek. Cross the creek and head upstream about 200 feet to the falls. The rocks can get slippery, and there is no established trail to the falls.

4.8 Arrive back at the trailhead.

12 Clikapudi Trail

Shasta Lake's premier day hike slinks along the waterfront through recent burn patches and light pine forest. The Clikapudi Trail is a 7.5-mile loop beginning and ending at the well-used Jones Valley Boat Launch on the lake's southern arm. Celebrated sights along the way include wide-open views, nesting bald eagles, and spring poppy blooms.

Distance: 7.5-mile loop
Approximate hiking time: 3 hours
Difficulty: Moderate
Trail surface: Dirt and rock path
Best season: Fall through spring
Other trail users: Mountain bikers, equestrians
Canine compatibility: Leashed dogs permitted
Fees and permits: None
Schedule: None
Maps: TOPO! California CD, Disc 3; USGS Bella Vista, CA; Shasta-Trinity National Forest's pamphlet: *Clikapudi Trail* (available online)
Trail contacts: Shasta-Trinity National Forest, Shasta Lake Visitor Center, 14250 Holiday Rd., Redding, CA 96003; (530) 275-1589; www.fs.fed.us/r5/shastatrinity
Special considerations: Hike is relatively exposed and can be subject to extreme summer heat

Finding the trailhead: From Redding take I-5 north about 5 miles to the Oasis Road exit (number 683) and head east. Drive 3.4 miles and turn right onto Bear Mountain Road. After 5.2 miles, make a left onto Dry Creek Road. Drive 1 mile and turn right at the sign for the Jones Valley Boat Launch (FR 33N03). The boat launch is 3.3 miles down FR 33N03 (a mile past the first Clikapudi trailhead) at N40 44.321' / W122 12.921'. Park at the gravel trailhead on your right just before the boat launch. You can also park at the paved boat-launch parking lot, but if you do, a day-use fee is required. If you are camping at nearby Jones Valley Campground, the trail at the end of the loop links with the Clikapudi Trail.

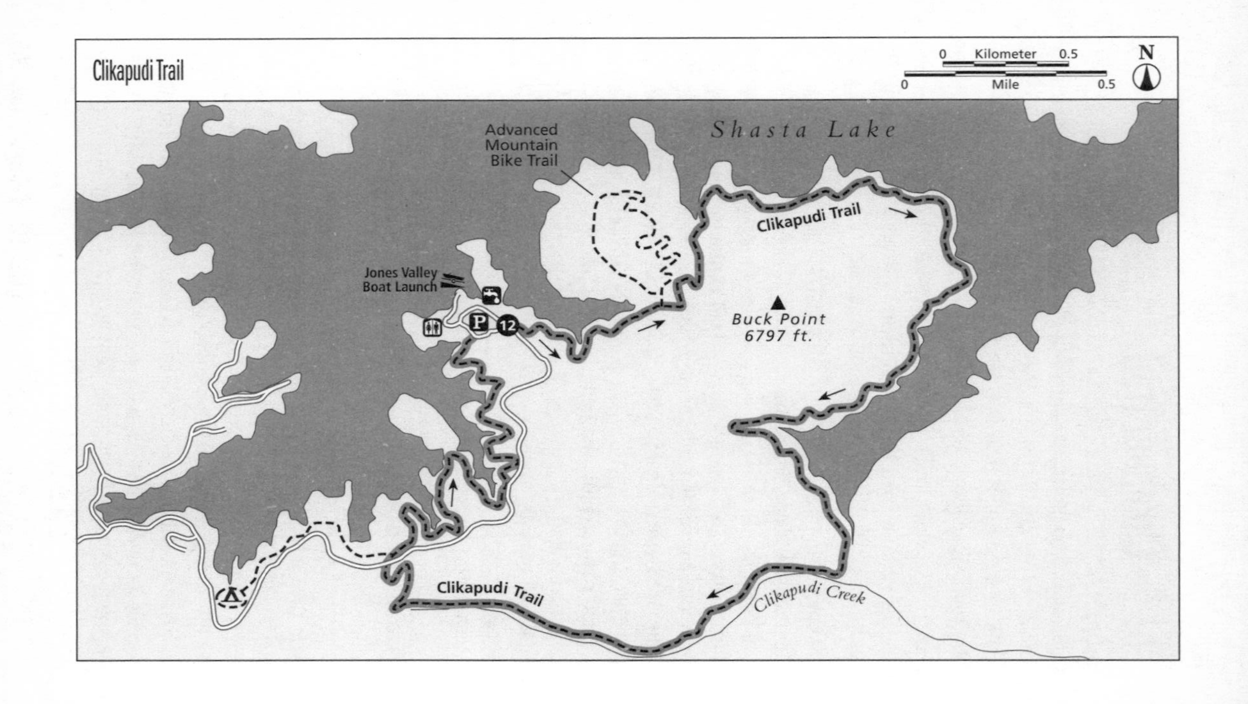
Clikapudi Trail
0 Kilometer 0.5
0 Mile 0.5
N
Shasta Lake
Advanced Mountain Bike Trail
Jones Valley Boat Launch
12
P
Clikapudi Trail
Buck Point 6797 ft.
Clikapudi Trail
Clikapudi Creek

The Hike

Clikapudi is a name derived from the Wintu word *klu-kupuda,* which means "kill." The unique title refers to a tragic battle of the 1800s between the local Wintu Native Americans and immigrant traders. Today the battlegrounds are part of Shasta Lake's national forest blanket, home to a variety of recreational uses. Nicknamed the Houseboat Capital of the World, Shasta Lake, along with the Jones Valley Boat Ramp, buzzes with summer boating activity. Hikers were allotted their own little piece of the area with the Clikapudi Trail.

In summer 2004, when the Bear Fire spread through the grounds, it had only been a mere four years since the previous burn, and the scalded land was left with little in the way of vegetation. It didn't, however, diminish the beauty of this trail, which now hosts widely unhindered views and particularly intense wildflower blooms. A few hearty pines even survived to tell the tale of the fires, and you can see their charred trunks on this hike.

The first few miles of the Clikapudi Trail largely follow the lakeshore, balancing slightly above the water on rolling ridges. Sprawling views of the turquoise water of the Pit Arm and hills beyond are never far from sight. The Jones Valley area is known as a hot spot for bald-eagle viewing. As you take your first steps along the Clikapudi Trail, heading east from the parking area, gaze up at those few mature tree-tops; it is not uncommon to see nests in these giants. Sadly, that is some of the last shadeworthy trees to be seen.

At 0.7 mile, the Advanced Mountain Bike Trail forks to the left. Around mile 3, the trail diverts from the water and follows a miniature valley paralleling Clikapudi Creek.

The scenery shifts to savanna-like grasslands until it finely zigzags up a hill (look for soaring raptors). After cresting the mound, you once again gaze upon the activities of Shasta Lake and the trailhead. When the trail descends, carefully watch for speeding traffic as you cross the road and head for the labeled continuum 200 yards to the right.

The spring wildflower blooms flourish in the nutrient-rich burn soils along the Clikapudi Trail. If you're nearby, it would be a shame to miss the carpet of lupine and California poppy in the spring. Dozens of other varieties of wildflowers sprout along the route as well, from shrubs like redbud and cinquefoil to such wildflowers as beaucoup shooting star and mariposa lily. *Mariposa* is Spanish for "butterfly," and the unique lilies of the Calochortus family are perfectly named as such. The spring azure, a petite periwinkle butterfly, nearly matches the mariposa petals it frequents. The small insects live only a week, but they flood this trail for those special few days. Also look for California tortoiseshell along with monarch and orange sulphur butterflies.

Miles and Directions

0.0 Begin at the trailhead east of the boat launch entrance. Follow the Clikapudi Trail east along a dirt path.

0.7 The Advanced Mountain Bike Trail forks left, stay right for Clikapudi Trail.

5.3 Reach FR 33N03. Carefully cross the road and head right for 200 yards to the signed trailhead to continue the loop.

7.5 Reach the boat-launch parking area. Arrive back at the trailhead at the eastern edge of the parking area.

13 Whiskeytown National Recreation Area: James K. Carr Trail (Whiskeytown Falls)

If you're ready for an adventure, then trek up to Whiskeytown Falls, but bring along a well-rested body and maybe even some energy bars for the climb. The 1.7-mile one-way trail hikes steadily up a decomposed granite path paralleling beautiful Crystal Creek, in Whiskeytown National Recreation Area. Just when you think you can't take another step up the 700-foot grade, you arrive at exhilarating Whiskeytown Falls, a large flow that crashes vigorously along a lengthy series of rocky rapids.

Distance: 3.4-mile out-and-back
Approximate hiking time: 2 hours
Difficulty: More challenging (due to steady uphill grade)
Trail surface: Decomposed granite path, rock stairs
Best season: Year-round
Other trail users: Mountain bikers, equestrians
Canine compatibility: Leashed dogs permitted
Fees and permits: Day-use fee
Schedule: Day use only
Maps: TOPO! California CD, Disc 2; USGS French Gulch, CA; Whiskeytown National Recreation Area's brochure: *James K. Carr Trail (Whiskeytown Falls)* (available online and at the visitor center)
Trail contacts: Whiskeytown National Recreation Area Visitor Center, CA 299 and Kennedy Memorial Drive, P.O. Box 188, Whiskeytown, CA 96095; (530) 246-1225 (visitor center) or (530) 242-3400 (park headquarters); www.nps.gov/whis
Special considerations: This trail can be closed in winter due to flooding and other hazards; always inquire with the land manager before you head out. There are no facilities at this trailhead.

Finding the trailhead: From downtown Redding at I-5, take the CA 299 exit west and follow CA 299 as it zig-zags through downtown then 8 miles past the outskirts of downtown to the Whiskeytown Visitor Center. After you've paid your park fees, pick up maps and information on the hike. Drive an additional 8 miles from the visitor center along CA 299 and turn left onto windy Crystal Creek Road. Drive 3.4 miles to the trailhead, on your left, at N40 38.273' / W122 40.557'.

The Hike

This hike for the hearty trudges steadily uphill through a mixed conifer forest to Whiskeytown National Recreation Area's awe-inspiring Whiskeytown Falls. The James K. Carr Trail is not a route for the weak, and although the word *easy* would be a stretch, this trail is definitely one of the best day hikes in the region.

It is hard to believe a waterfall of Whiskeytown's thunderous magnitude could ever have been forgotten, but this landmark was in fact recently "rediscovered." The beautiful cascade had been left to the wilds for over half a century until park employees stumbled upon the flow during the exploration of the Crystal Creek drainage in 2004. A unique attraction such as this couldn't lay isolated for long, and by 2005 construction of the trail had begun. The trail's name commemorates James K. Carr, a Redding resident instrumental to the development of the recreation area.

The hike begins along an old road converted to trail in a stand of ponderosa pines. After a quick 0.5 mile downhill the Crystal Creek crossing comes into view. In 2009 the footbridge was carried away during a flood—a testament to the many hazards that this route is subject to. Fires of the previous summer had decimated tons of native brush, and even though these fires are a natural part of the ecosystem, the lack of small, sturdy shrubs exposed soils to erosion. Combining the loose dirt with heavy rains produced the potential for mudslides. Many of the park's trails, including Whiskeytown Falls, were subject to closures. Always check the status of this route in the wet months.

After the creek crossing, the trail quickly narrows into the track you'll follow to the falls. Views of Mount Shasta and Clear Creek mesh with the pine, buckeye and oak that edge the system. Spring blooms produce many of the usual suspects, including lupine, iris, poppy, phlox, sunflower, and buttercup. Several small social trails fork to the side, some diverting down to the water and others merely wandering logging spurs.

Patience wins the prize on this hike for those who take it slow and steady up the 700-foot elevation gain. The decomposed granite footing can be slick, so choose sturdy hiking boots with a gripping outsole for this journey. A picnic area is conveniently stationed 1.5 miles in, lending a catch-your-breath excuse for the weary. After that is a short jaunt under a 0.5 mile along the crisp creek to the falls.

Once you reach the trail's end, the view is dramatic. Whiskeytown Falls is a large and powerful waterfall that flows strongly throughout the year. The refreshing force splashes into a deep pool below its final drop, where you might even see a brave local daring to dip in the frigid waters. This first view of the stout falls and pool only tells half the story; a more compelling picture lies above. Follow the rock steps to the left for a bird's-eye-view of the rapids feeding the drop. Be sure to clench that guardrail up the slick rock steps.

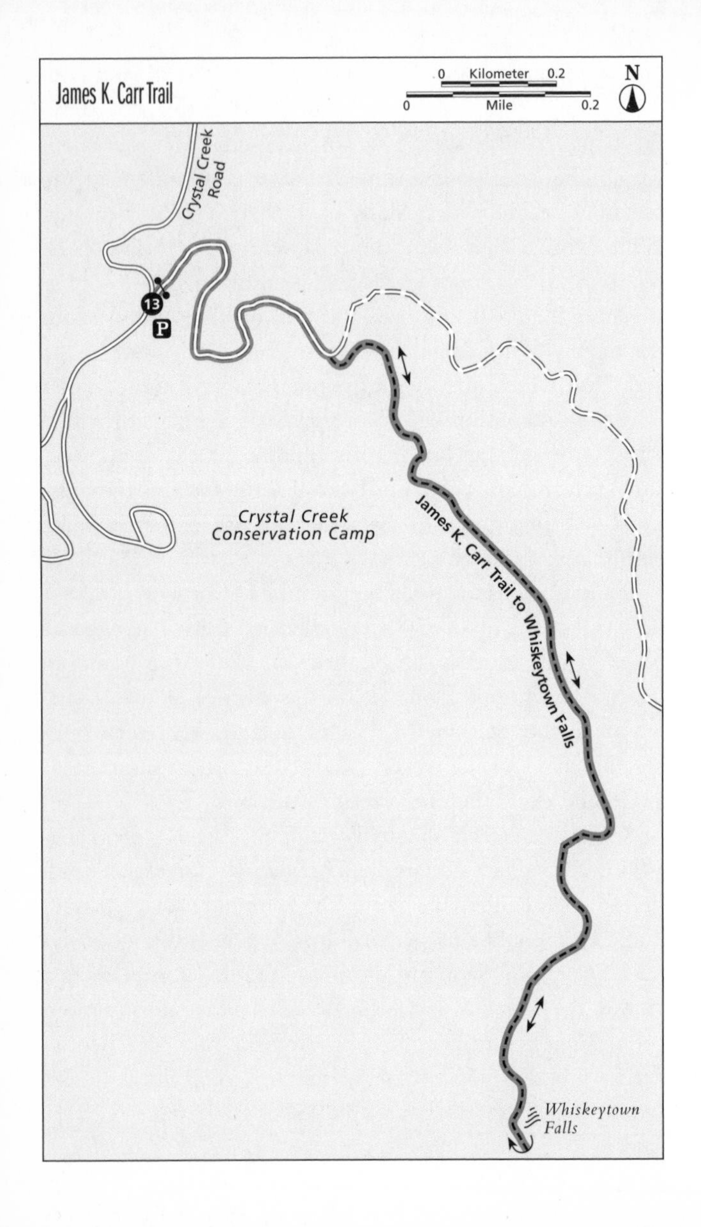

James K. Carr Trail
0 Kilometer 0.2
0 Mile 0.2
N
Crystal Creek Road
13
P
Crystal Creek Conservation Camp
James K. Carr Trail to Whiskeytown Falls
Whiskeytown Falls

Miles and Directions

0.0 From the parking area, head east, following the trail downhill.

0.1 Cross Crystal Creek.

0.5 A social spur trail on the left leads to a creek. Stay to the right for the Whiskeytown Falls Trail.

1.5 Reach the picnic area.

1.7 Arrive at the falls. The steep rock steps on the left lead to the falls overlook.

3.4 Backtrack to arrive at the trailhead.

14 Whiskeytown National Recreation Area: Camden Water Ditch Trail

This easy hike for history buffs trails through a gold-rush-era ranch in Whiskeytown National Recreation Area's Tower House Historic District. The grounds are complete with an old farmhouse, apple orchard, and historic grave site. The easy 1.3-mile loop follows the defunct Camden water ditch and has interpretive displays.

Distance: 1.3-mile loop
Approximate hiking time: 1 hour
Difficulty: Easy
Trail surface: Gravel and dirt path
Best season: Year-round
Other trail users: None
Canine compatibility: Leashed dogs permitted
Fees and permits: Day-use fee
Schedule: None
Maps: TOPO! California CD, Disc 2; USGS French Gulch, CA; Whiskeytown National Recreation Area's brochure: *Camden Water Ditch Trail* (available online and at the visitor center)
Trail contacts: Whiskeytown National Recreation Area Visitor Center, CA 299 and Kennedy Memorial Drive, P.O. Box 188, Whiskeytown, CA 96095; (530) 246-1225 (visitor center) or (530) 242-3400 (park headquarters); www.nps.gov/whis
Special considerations: There is no water at this trailhead.

Finding the trailhead: From I-5 in downtown Redding, take the CA 299 exit west and follow CA 299 as it zig-zags through downtown then 8 miles past the outskirts of downtown to the Whiskeytown Visitor Center. After you've paid your park fees and picked up maps and information, head left on CA 299 from the parking area and drive 7.8 miles to the Tower House Historic District and the trailhead on the left at N40 39.813' / W122 38.064'.

The Hike

Whiskeytown is thick in history. The area is packed with stories of water wars, tragic battles with local Native Americans, high-impact mining operations, and rowdy camps. With a name like Whiskeytown, it is easy to assume that the words *whiskey* and *town* can only mean one thing—yup, gold mining!

Whiskeytown was once a thriving 1850s gold-rush community, made strong for a time by the rich gravels of the area's streams and rivers. Today the town's remnants are buried beneath a 3,000-acre reservoir that is popular for boating, fishing, and camping. For a crash course on the history and nature of the region, consider hiking the 0.4-mile interpretive loop at the Whiskeytown National Recreation Area's visitor center. This trail is the perfect way to start exploring the park and leads to the lakeshore (bring your suit for the swimming beach).

After you've paid your dues at the visitor center, continue the park tour along the Camden Water Ditch Trail in the Tower House Historic District. The cluster of original gold-rush era ranches is located about 8 miles west along CA 299. From the parking area you can pick up the Camden Water Ditch Trail by following the briefly paved path over a couple Clear Creek footbridges and heading south for a clockwise loop. The Camden Water Ditch Trail follows the historic canal that once carried diverted water to area orchards. The hike largely wanders through scattered oaks and blackberry bushes with glimpses of the Camden House and Willow Creek.

Interpretive signs take hikers on a journey back in time, telling stories of the main landholders of the district. One

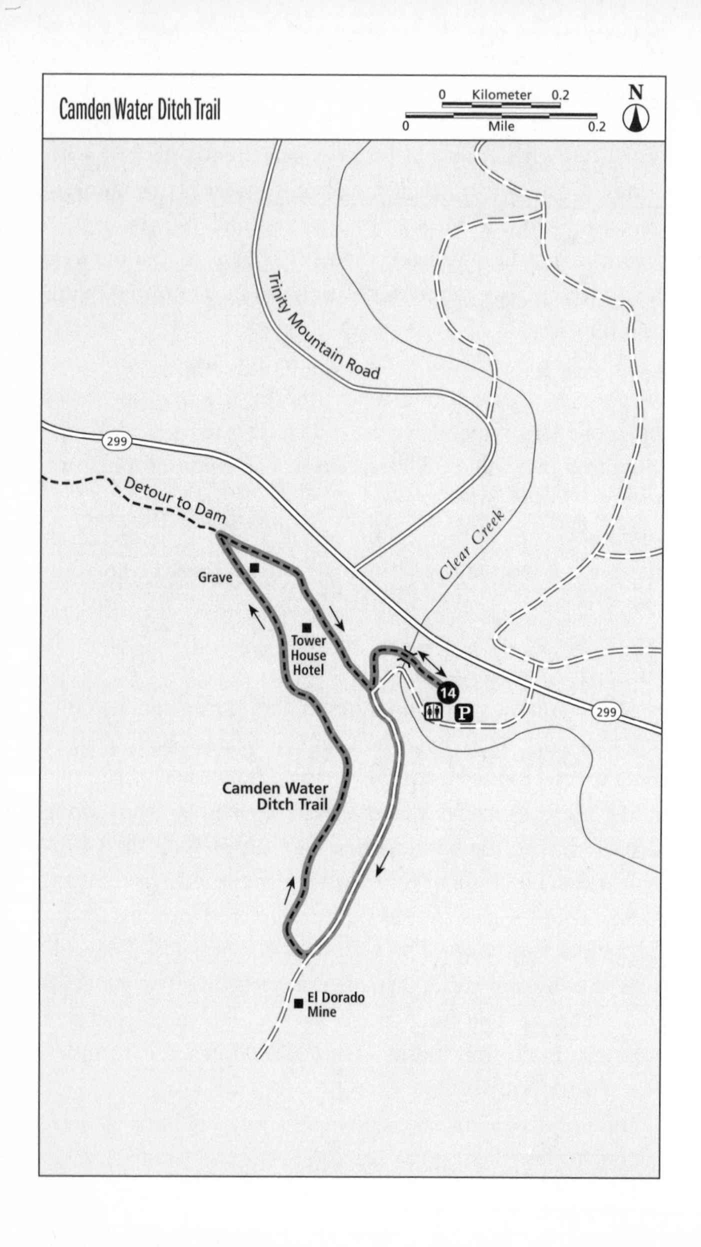
Camden Water Ditch Trail
0 Kilometer 0.2
0 Mile 0.2
N
Trinity Mountain Road
299
Detour to Dam
Clear Creek
Grave
Tower
House
Hotel
14
P
299
Camden Water
Ditch Trail
El Dorado
Mine

landmark is the grave site of Levi Tower, the proprietor of the Tower House Hotel. At the grave, the trail continues through some original fruit trees. Back on the loop, the trail curves again, passing by the old Camden House barn and caretaker's house, which is now a National Park Service housing. For a quick extension, consider the Mill Creek Trail which leads to the remnants of the El Dorado Mine. If you decide to hop on the Mill Creek Trail, be sure to pick up a copy of the trail guide at the visitor center.

Miles and Directions

0.0 From the trailhead begin on a paved path heading west. After about 300 feet cross the pedestrian bridge over Clear Creek. Known as the Toll Bridge, this relic was built in 1865.

0.1 A fork in the trail leads to a dead-end at the old hotel, follow the Camden Water Ditch Trail and signs for El Dorado Mine to a second footbridge over Clear Creek.

0.3 Pass an the old farmhouse, follow the trail left along the creek for a clockwise loop.

0.5 Camden Water Ditch Trail goes right, and the Mill Creek Trail to the El Dorado Mine leads ahead. Stay on the Camden Trail passing through a small open meadow.

0.9 Turn right at the gravesite following the Camden Water Ditch Trail east through the old apple orchard.

1.1 Go left to pass back over the second footbridge.

1.2 Pass back over the toll bridge.

1.3 Arrive back at the trailhead.

15 Whiskeytown National Recreation Area: Oak Bottom Water Ditch Trail

Oak Bottom Water Ditch Trail is a nice cool route in Whiskeytown National Recreation Area. The waterfront walk diverts through shady manzanita hollows along Whiskeytown Lake. In the hot months, pack the swimsuits and take a quick dip along the shallow beaches, or bring a fishing pole and take full advantage of this waterside location.

Distance: 5-mile out-and-back
Approximate hiking time: 2 hours
Difficulty: Easy
Trail surface: Dirt path
Best season: Year-round
Other trail users: Mountain bikers, equestrians
Canine compatibility: Leashed dogs permitted
Fees and permits: Day-use fee
Schedule: Day use only
Maps: TOPO! California CD, Disc 2; USGS Whiskeytown, CA; Whiskeytown National Recreation Area's brochure: *Oak Bottom Water Ditch Trail* (available online and at the visitor center)
Trail contacts: Whiskeytown National Recreation Area Visitor Center, CA 299 and Kennedy Memorial Drive, P.O. Box 188, Whiskeytown, CA 96095; (530) 246-1225 (visitor center) or (530) 242-3400 (park headquarters); www.nps.gov/whis
Special considerations: No facilities directly at this trailhead; stop by the campground for restrooms and water

Finding the trailhead: From I-5 in downtown Redding, take the CA 299 exit west and follow CA 299 as it zig-zags through downtown then 8 miles past the outskirts of downtown to the Whiskeytown Visitor Center. After you've paid your park fees and picked up maps and information, head left back onto CA 299 for an additional 5 miles and turn left at the signs for the Oak Bottom Campground. The trailhead is on your right at N40 39.039' / W122 35.655', before the campground or other area facilities.

The Hike

The Oak Bottom Water Ditch Trail is an excellent summer option, cool and shady even when it seems the heat has driven away hope for a friendly day hike. Protection of manzanita tunnels, rock walls, and knobcone pine shade the trail. The route follows Whiskeytown Lake's shoreline, and on a lucky summer day heavy gusts pick up a cooler breeze across the water. Social trails and a bit of bushwhacking lead to several swimming beaches (don't expect smooth sand; pack a pair of water shoes).

The history of the trail predates the man-made lake. The dirt path was once a gold-rush-era canal system designed to haul water to Clear Creek–area mining operations nearly one hundred years before the lake was created. Coincidentally, the route conveniently traverses today's lake, almost with precision. As you walk through the shaded groves and along the cool water's edge, occasional boats and kayaks cruise by, and anglers wade the shore in search of trout, bass, and catfish.

The trail diverts away from the serene scene and buddies up to CA 299 along the 0.5-mile mark. This is the only time the hike is fairly exposed, to both the elements and the sound of traffic, so gaze up at the lovely rounded mountains to your left. The 6,209-foot Shasta Bally peaks over the brush, drizzled in snow often through spring.

Once the journey creeps away from the blazing highway, keep an eye peeled for lake-loving wildlife. You might spy one of the park's 160-plus species of birds, 13 species of bats, 13 species of snakes, 7 kinds of lizards, or the 1

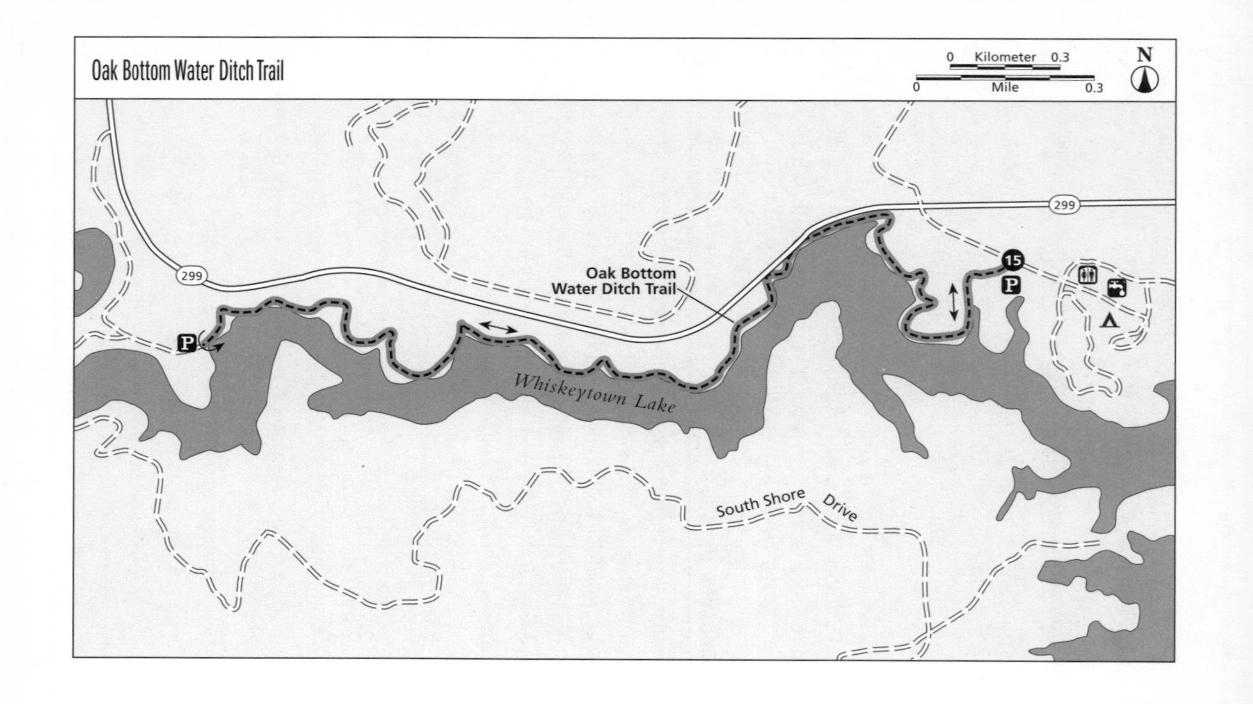
Oak Bottom Water Ditch Trail
0 Kilometer 0.3
0 Mile 0.3
N
299
299
15
P
P
Oak Bottom
Water Ditch Trail
Whiskeytown Lake
South Shore Drive

kind of turtle, the western pond turtle. These turtles can be frequently viewed from this trail, resting on lakeshore logs in this desirable habitat. Study the shore closely; the slim brown shells are easy to overlook. For a full species list of the amazingly diverse plants and animals that can be seen along area trails, stop by the visitor center.

The trail abruptly ends at an area known as the Carr Powerhouse, which offers a primitive parking area off an unlabeled gravel road. This would make a nice circuit for a 2.5-mile hike one-way, but you would have to organize transport; otherwise it's a breezy backtrack to the original trailhead.

Miles and Directions

0.0 From the trailhead, follow Oak Bottom Water Ditch Trail southwest and then west along the lakeshore, by staying right at the first intersection (going left leads along the lakeshore toward the campground).

1.6 After a small footbridge, social paths lead left to swimming beaches, continue west along the Oak Bottom Water Ditch Trail.

1.8 Pass by a gate and cross a dirt road, following the trail signs directing the trail to the right past the road.

2.5 Reach the Carr Powerhouse. Backtrack from here.

5.0 Arrive back at the trailhead.

16 Hornbeck and Sacramento Ditch Trails

The Hornbeck Trail has it all—urban proximity, spanning vistas, swimming beaches, wildlife, and peaceful benches under shady ancient oaks. Perhaps Redding's premier wilderness hike, the trail follows an old railroad bed across a ridge sharply cut into hillsides and then softly swoops through manzanita groves. The Sacramento Ditch Trail replaces Hornbeck Trail north of Walker Mine Road, where it parallels the handsome Sacramento River atop a high rim to Shasta Dam.

Distance: 8-mile out-and-back (with shorter and longer options)
Approximate hiking time: 4 hours
Difficulty: Moderate
Trail surface: Dirt and rock path, old railroad bed
Best season: Year-round
Other trail users: Mountain bikers, equestrians
Canine compatibility: Leashed dogs permitted
Fees and permits: None
Schedule: Day use only
Maps: TOPO! California CD, Disc 2; USGS Shasta Dam, CA; Bureau of Land Management's leaflet: *Hornbeck Trail* (available at Walker Mine Road trailhead); Shasta County Public Health Department's brochure: *Redding Walks* (available at BLM)
Trail contacts: Bureau of Land Management, Redding Field Office, 355 Hemsted Dr., Redding, CA 96002; (530) 224-2100; www.blm.gov/ca/redding
Special considerations: There are no facilities at this trailhead. This trail is fairly exposed and subject to extreme summer heat; if hiking during the hot summer months, consider traveling this route closer to dawn or dusk.

Finding the trailhead: The Hornbeck and Sacramento Ditch Trails are located east of downtown Redding, just across the river. From I-5 in central Redding, take the CA 299 East/Lake Boulevard exit (680) west. Follow Lake Boulevard west for 3 miles and turn left onto Quartz Hill Road. Drive 1 mile to the Quartz Hill Road Trailhead, on your right, at N40 38.155' / W122 25.290'.

The Hike

The Hornbeck Trail is one of Redding's most popular city escapes. The easy-to-navigate journey moves along the eastern edge of Keswick Reservoir, not far from central Redding. The track is the once-forgotten and long-defunct railroad route used to haul quartz from Quartz Hill Mine for copper smelting during the gold-rush era. The historic track was once known as Old Diggings Railroad and was renamed Hornbeck to commemorate one of the many volunteers who were influential to the route's reincarnation. You might still find local trail legend Chuck Hornbeck leading historical tours along this very trail as part of the Shasta Historical Society's Hikes for Health and History.

There are a half dozen parking areas where you can jump on and off well-labeled Hornbeck and Sacramento Ditch Trails, and another half dozen routes that could be created from the system. In its entirety, the Hornbeck Trail runs 4 miles each direction out-and-back from Walker Mine Road to Quartz Hill Road. The Lower Sacramento Ditch Trail runs roughly parallel to the Hornbeck Trail along an old water ditch, and a loop can be created in a combination of the two. The Upper Sacramento Ditch Trail moves north from Walker Mine Road in opposing direction from the reservoir and follows the Sacramento River. The trail is perched several hundred feet above the water on a rolling track with lovely canyon views. After 9 scenic miles from Walker Mine Road, the Upper Sacramento Ditch Trail concludes (or begins) at Shasta Dam.

The Hornbeck Trail probably gets the most hiking action of Redding and poses the perfect out-and-back day hike. If you begin at the Quartz Hill Road Trailhead, you can pick up a map at the parking area and head out on the slim single track. As you travel through the manzanita stands, take note of the stout, low-profile steel trail markers. These handy indicators are used to identify all major intersections and will guide you in whatever direction your day goes.

The majority of the Hornbeck Trail runs above Keswick Reservoir, the body of water diverted from the Sacramento River. The reservoir, which looks like a wide river channel, is a popular trout-fishing hole and is designed to seasonally trap salmon. A few concrete benches are located along the way and overlook the water. At 2.6 miles, an access trail leads to the shore. At this point you can also head right and create a loop with the Lower Sacramento Ditch Trail. Roughly a mile later on the Hornbeck Trail, a quick spur trail to the left leads to Freita's Point. The reservoir overlook is based around old concrete pilings that were part of a tramway that carried ore down the mountain.

Back on track, Hornbeck Trail moves away from the water through healthy oak, manzanita, and chaparral. At the 4-mile mark, Hornbeck Trail hits Walker Mine Road and a small trailhead. From there you will have to retrace your steps back to the Quartz Hill Road Trailhead.

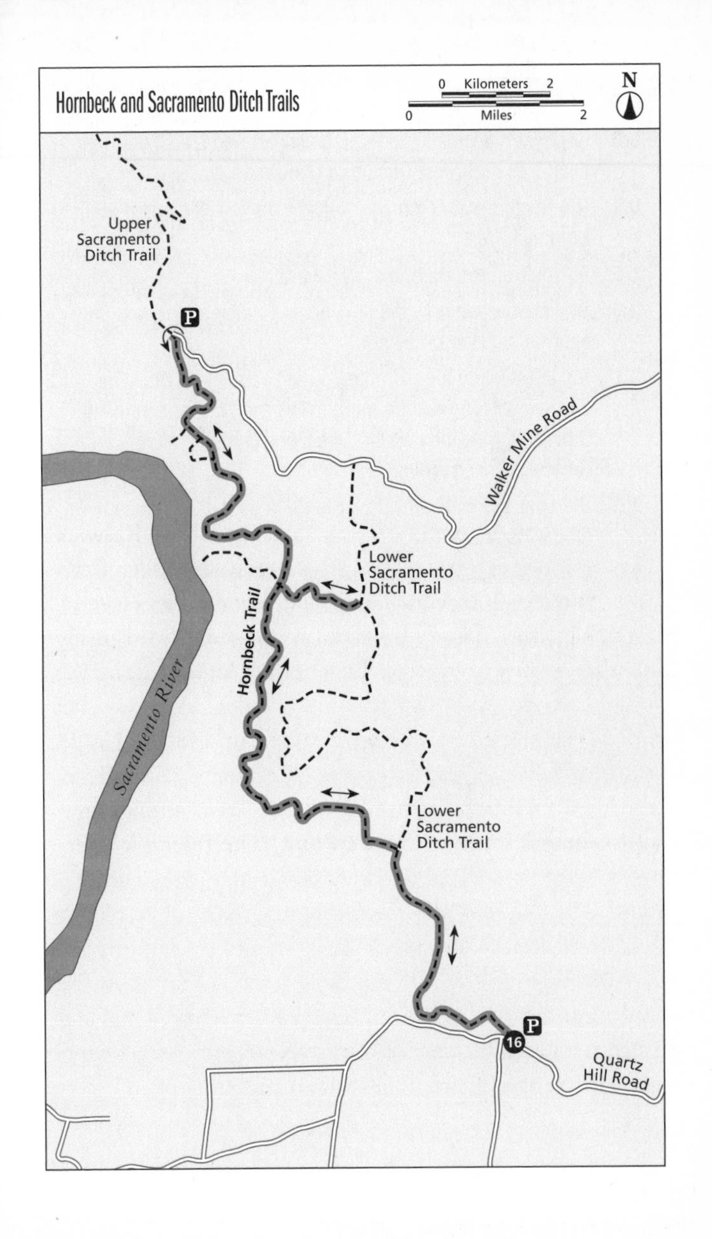
Hornbeck and Sacramento Ditch Trails
0 Kilometers 2
0 Miles 2
N
Upper Sacramento Ditch Trail
P
Walker Mine Road
Lower Sacramento Ditch Trail
Hornbeck Trail
Sacramento River
Lower Sacramento Ditch Trail
P
16
Quartz Hill Road

Miles and Directions

0.0 Begin at the Quartz Hill Road Trailhead and follow the Hornbeck Trail northwest through a manzanita grove.

0.7 The Sacramento Ditch Trail forks to the left. Stay right on the Hornbeck Trail.

1.0 Stay left on the Hornbeck Trail.

2.6 The intersection with the lake access trail is to the left. Stay right on the Hornbeck Trail.

2.7 A Y intersection leads to the Lower Sacramento Ditch Trail on the right. To create a loop, follow the Lower Sacramento Ditch Trail east then south. Directions continue along the Hornbeck Trail heading north.

3.5 The spur trail to Freita's Point forks to the left, continue north on the Hornbeck Trail.

4.0 End at Walker Mine Road and the trailhead for the Upper Sacramento Ditch Trail (no facilities). Backtrack from here.

8.0 Arrive back at the Quartz Hill Road Trailhead.

17 Lema Ranch and Churn Creek Trails

When you need a breath of fresh air but aren't up to driving out of town, head for the Lema Ranch and Churn Creek system, where you can choose from two distinctively different styles of hike. Lema Ranch hosts a perfectly polished paved path through an old farm with plenty of ponds and a persimmon grove. The more organic flavor of Churn Creek's rolling oak lands allows dogs and cyclists along its gravel paths. Both systems offer excellent birding.

Distance: 2.2-mile loop (with longer options)
Approximate hiking time: 1 hour
Difficulty: Easy
Trail surface: Paved, gravel
Best season: Year-round
Other trail users: Mountain bikers on Churn Creek trails
Canine compatibility: Leashed dogs permitted on Churn Creek trails; dogs not permitted on Lema Ranch trails
Fees and permits: None
Schedule: Trails closed from dusk until dawn
Maps: TOPO! California CD, Disc 2; USGS Enterprise, CA; Shasta County Public Health Department's brochure: *Redding Walks* (available at BLM); the McConnell Foundation's brochure: *Trails* (available online)
Trail contacts: The McConnell Foundation, 800 Shasta View Dr., Redding, CA 96003; (530) 226-6200; www.mcconnellfoundation.org; Bureau of Land Management, Redding Field Office, 355 Hemsted Dr., Redding, CA 96002; (530) 224-2100; www.blm.gov/ca/redding
Special considerations: Restrooms and water are not available at all trailheads. There are many ways to enter this trail.

Finding the trailhead: From I-5 in Redding take CA 299 East/Lake Boulevard exit (680) east and take the first exit onto Churn Creek Road south. Make an immediate left onto College View Road.

Drive 0.7 mile and turn right onto Shasta View Drive. After 1 mile, turn left onto Hemingway Street. The trailhead is tucked away on the immediate left at N40 36.144' / W122 19.966'.

The Hike

The McConnell Foundation, a Redding icon, has been operating since the mid-1980s, and is responsible for dozens of community development projects in the region and beyond. Thanks to the generous philanthropy of Carl and Leah McConnell, the foundation has dispersed over $100 million in grants and showered their hometown of Redding with assets, including several beautiful trails and an up-and-coming art college.

Lema Ranch is home base for the McConnell Foundation and the premier walking trail of Redding. Lema Ranch trails total a little over 4 pristine paved miles, splicing through possibly the most well-maintained ranch to ever have been preserved. With a maintenance team working daily, zooming around the perfectly manicured lawns, there is almost a golf-course feel to this urban route. You can pick up the system at several locations; many include restrooms with flush toilets and water facilities. The wide, even trails are open solely to hikers, joggers, and walkers; they are closed to cyclists, skaters, and dogs. Smoking, swimming, and fishing are not permitted.

The system is set up in a large loop with smaller loop options within. The Mule Loop Trail, detailed in Miles and Directions, is the heart of the system. The trail centers the property, offering access to each smaller option, and meanders past several large ponds thick in swooning willows. You will also find pastures, geese, old farm equipment, and a persimmon orchard on the tour. The ranch is a simple and lovely place to take a slow stroll, with Redding's signature backdrop of majestic mountain peaks.

Every 0.25 mile or so, a bench peers over another scenic section of the ranch; several edge the peaceful ponds, encouraging birders to stay longer. Bring the binoculars, and you might catch the western bluebird hopping by the trail, or many water-loving species such as heron, egret, ring-necked duck, moorhen, and great-tailed grackle. If you decide to bird here, contact the Wintu Audubon Society (www.wintuaudubon.org) for a full species list.

Churn Creek is another beautiful trail system that connects to the north end of Lema Ranch. The extrawide gravel trail rolls over grassy hills through valiant oak groves and is open to cycling as well as dog walking. Spring is a nice time to hit this site, when the seasonal waterways trickle with life. Waterfowl, along with sparrows, blackbirds, woodpeckers, and hawks, may fly by. Much like Lema Ranch, several trailheads link to the outer loop that roots the Churn Creek Trail. These trailheads don't have the facilities of the Lema Ranch trailheads, so if you're traveling on foot without a canine companion in tow, you might want to park at the main Lema Ranch trailhead just off Shasta View Drive and head north for Churn Creek trails.

Miles and Directions

0.0 Beginning at the main trailhead, head counterclockwise, following the signs for the Mule Loop near the restrooms.

0.1 The Secluded Loop is to the left; stay right for the Mule Loop.

0.5 Access links to the left lead to the Churn Creek trail system; stay right for the Mule Loop.

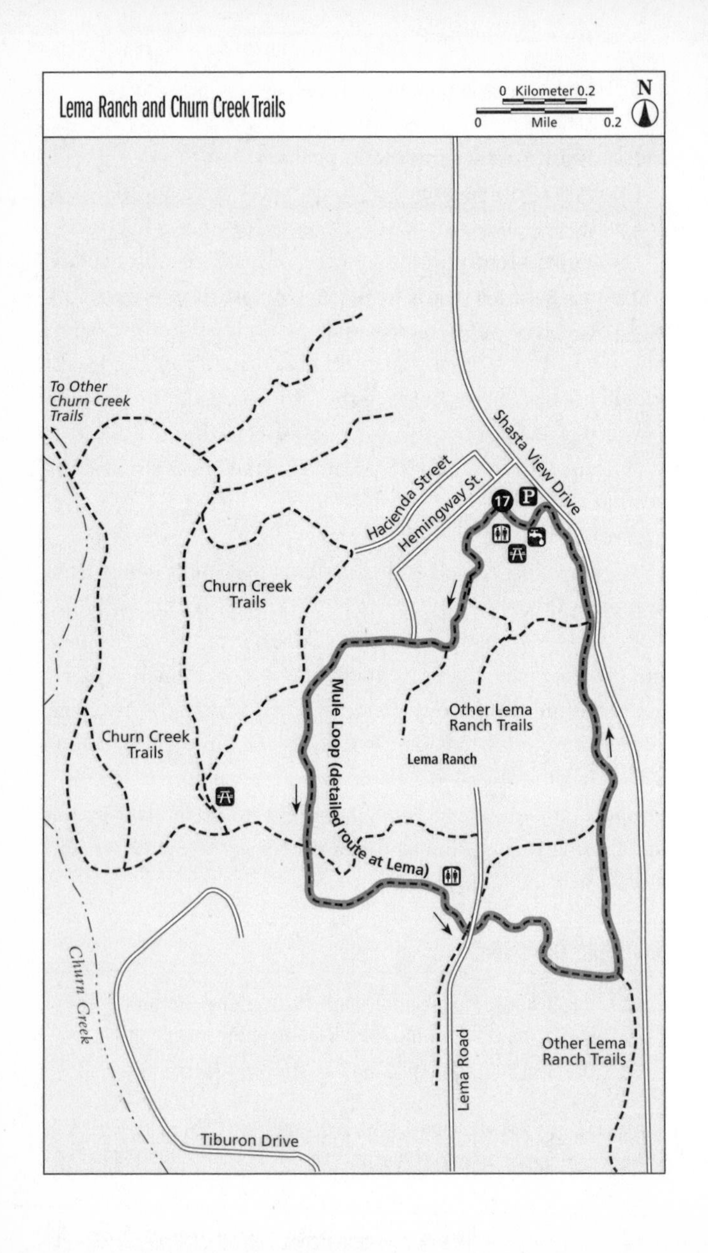
Lema Ranch and Churn Creek Trails
0 Kilometer 0.2
0 Mile 0.2
N
To Other Churn Creek Trails
Shasta View Drive
Hacienda Street
Hemingway St.
17
P
Churn Creek Trails
Other Lema Ranch Trails
Mule Loop (detailed route at Lema)
Lema Ranch
Churn Creek Trails
Churn Creek
Lema Road
Other Lema Ranch Trails
Tiburon Drive

0.7 Leah Loop diverts to the right; stay straight for the Mule Loop.

1.1 Reach a set of restrooms.

1.5 Stay left for the Mule Loop.

1.7 An intersection with the Leah Loop is to the left, stay right for Mule Loop.

2.0 The Secluded Loop is to the left, stay right for Mule Loop.

2.2 Arrive back at the trailhead.

18 Sacramento River and Rail Trails

The Sacramento River Trail is the pride and joy of Redding, and rightfully so. This masterpiece of a hike leads to the phenomenal Sundial Bridge, an architectural trophy over the Sacramento River. You can begin the route at the Turtle Bay Exploration Park, which is home to a day's worth of activities in itself. The other 12 miles of the River Trail get up close and personal with life in the riparian zone. You may spy river otters, beavers, and dozens of shorebirds along the trail's wide paved paths. If you're still ready for more, hop on the adjoining Rail Trail and follow the gravel route clear up to Shasta Dam.

Distance: 8-mile loop (with shorter and longer options)
Approximate hiking time: 4 hours
Difficulty: Easy
Trail surface: Paved on Sacramento River Trail; dirt and gravel path on Sacramento Rail Trail
Best season: Year-round
Other trail users: Joggers and cyclists on Sacramento River Trail; equestrians and mountain bikers on Sacramento Rail Trail
Canine compatibility: Leashed dogs permitted
Fees and permits: None
Schedule: Day use only on Sacramento River and Rail Trails; Sundial Bridge open 6 a.m. to midnight
Maps: TOPO! California CD, Disc 2; Shasta County Public Health Department's brochure: *Redding Walks* (available at BLM, Bureau of Land Management's brochure: *Sacramento River Rail Trail*)
Trail contacts: City of Redding, Community Services Department, 777 Cypress Ave., Redding, CA 96001; (530) 225-4512; www.reddingtrails.com; Bureau of Land Management, Redding Field Office, 355 Hemsted Dr., Redding, CA 96002; (530) 224-2100; www.blm.gov/ca/redding

Special considerations: This route is rapidly being developed and upgraded; contact the appropriate land managers for the most current maps

Finding the trailhead: You can't miss Redding's Sundial Bridge; even the highway exit is labeled after it. There are a dozen ways to access these trails, including several popular parking areas. The main parking lot for the Sacramento River Trail is just a few footsteps from the Sundial Bridge at Turtle Bay. To reach the Turtle Bay parking area from I-5, take CA 44 west 0.7 mile to exit 1 Sundial Bridge. Turn right into Turtle Bay Exploration Park and follow the signs for the Sundial Bridge parking on the left at N40 35.455' / W122 22.671'.

The Hike

It would be a shame to not make a day (or two!) out of touring the Sacramento River and Rail Trails. The connecting routes are part of the Sacramento River Parkway, which stretches 60 miles in total from Shasta Dam to Red Bluff, encompassing over 65,000 acres and 45 miles of growing trails. In the last couple of decades, over $85 million has been dedicated to the creation and expansion of this phenomenal preserve.

The Sacramento River is California's longest river, beginning north of Redding and stretching clear to San Francisco Bay. The sensitive system of sloughs and lush forest along the river's banks are known as the riparian forest. At one point there was over a half million acres of this pristine landscape, but today less than 5 percent of the habitat remains. The Redding region's Sacramento River hosts an irreplaceable ecosystem for the plants and animals who survive solely in this precious environment. The desirability of the land is apparent on this trail, which offers some of

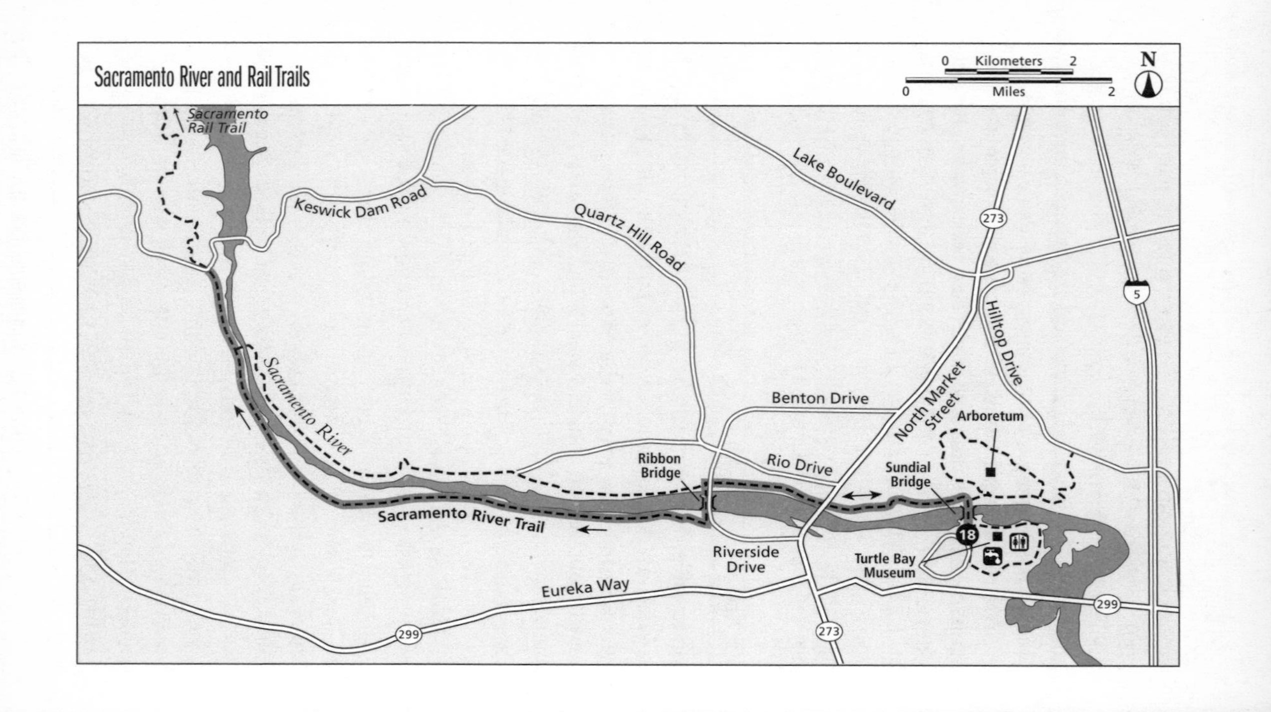
Sacramento River and Rail Trails
0 Kilometers 2
0 Miles 2
N
Sacramento Rail Trail
Keswick Dam Road
Quartz Hill Road
Lake Boulevard
273
5
Hilltop Drive
North Market Street
Benton Drive
Arboretum
Sacramento River
Ribbon Bridge
Rio Drive
Sundial Bridge
Sacramento River Trail
18
Riverside Drive
Turtle Bay Museum
Eureka Way
299
273
299

the most accessible wildlife viewing in the region. While en route you may encounter some of the nearly 300 kinds of animals who thrive in this zone. Regular characters include river otters and beavers, herons, egrets, pelicans, cormorants, and dozens of species of migratory birds and songbirds.

Most will begin their initial explorations of the Sacramento River Trail at Turtle Bay, an impressive city-operated ecology park home to the Turtle Bay Museum and Arboretum. The park spans 300 acres, stretching across the river and connected by the phenomenal Sundial Bridge. Resurrected in 2004 at a whopping cost of $23 million, the world-renowned bridge was designed by Spanish architect Santiago Calatrava. The cable-stayed structure is held by a 217-foot-tall sundial, said to be the largest in the world. The undeniably dramatic dial is only perfectly accurate on the solstice, although you can watch the shadow travel at a rate of 1 foot per hour on a daily basis.

If you headed north from the Turtle Bay trailhead, going upstream after crossing the Sundial Bridge, you would travel about 6 paved miles before meeting with the gravel Sacramento Rail Trail, which stretches another 9 miles along the river's western bank to Shasta Dam. When you cross the 700-foot-long bridge, you will be standing at the base of the dial. The amazing footpath is luminescent at night with blue and green hues reflected off the water through the thick frosted glass. Yet, at any time of day, there is usually a crowd standing in awe against the glory of the bleached white bridge. Why not stop as well and have a gander at this engineering marvel?

After you've paid homage to the dial, you can head right or left along the paved River Trail, which also lines this eastern side of the river. A quick jaunt to the right will link to the Arboretum Loop. If you combine this hike with a day at the impressive Turtle Bay Museum, you will have had a good taste of the 300-acre park. Another day you might head upstream to the Sacramento Rail Trail, which begins fairly high above the river and slinks along a similar ridge as the Sacramento Ditch Trail. It's an old rail line abandoned since the 1980s and now converted to an extra wide gravel road, a chunk of which is even open to motorized vehicles in the Copley Mountain staging area of the Chappie-Shasta OHV.

Miles and Directions

0.0 Beginning at Turtle Bay, begin the Sacramento River Trail by heading north across the Sacramento River.

0.2 Arrive at Sundial Bridge and the sundial, on the north side of the river and continue the hike west past the arboretum.

1.3 Turn left, heading south across the Diestelhorst Bridge. Follow the trail right, heading upstream (west) along the river.

4.0 Turn right to cross Ribbon Bridge, going north over the river. Continue east on the trail towards the Sundial Bridge. If you continued the hike north instead of crossing the river, you would reach the Sacramento Rail Trail.

7.8 Return to the Sundial Bridge, head south across the bridge to reach Turtle Bay.

8.0 Arrive back at the Turtle Bay trailhead.

19 Westside Trail to Salt Creek

The natural, yet urban, Westside Trail offers a wilderness feel within Redding city lines. This easy route showcases the region's best—mountain views, peaceful Salt Creek, and rocky hills dotted with oaks and pines.

Distance: 3-mile out-and-back (with longer options)
Approximate hiking time: 1.5 hours
Difficulty: Easy
Trail surface: Dirt path
Best season: Year-round
Other trail users: Mountain bikers, equestrians
Canine compatibility: Leashed dogs permitted
Fees and permits: None
Schedule: Day use only
Maps: TOPO! California CD, Disc 2; USGS Redding, CA; Shasta County Public Health Department's brochure: Redding Walks (available at BLM)
Trail contacts: Bureau of Land Management, Redding Field Office, 355 Hemsted Dr., Redding, CA 96002; (530) 224-2100; www.blm.gov/ca/redding
Special considerations: There are no restrooms at this trailhead. Much of the trail is adjacent to private property; always stay on the established trail.

Finding the trailhead: From central Redding take CA 299 exit west and follow it as it zig-zags through downtown for a little over 5 miles and turn left, heading southwest, onto Lower Springs Road. Drive 0.7 mile to the small gravel parking area on the left at the intersection of Lower Springs Road and Valparaiso Way, at N40 34.580' / W122 27.347'.

The Hike

True to their outdoors enthusiasm, the community of Redding really came together to develop the Westside Trail. The

Trails and Bikeway Council, City of Redding, Bureau of Land Management, California Conservation Corps, McConnell Foundation, as well as private contributors and dozens of volunteers are all responsible for the birth of the Westside Trail, which links several miles of western Redding.

The system continues to grow almost daily, with fresh loops and spurs being added and new land contributed to the project. Be sure to stop and pick up the most updated copy of the trail map at the Redding Bureau of Land Management office before your Westside adventure. Most trails are unlabeled and rustic, dropping and climbing a high ridge above the city. But just like the route itself, this is likely to change in the future.

The route along Salt Creek is one of the latest additions to the Westside Trail, popping up in spring 2009. Although the trail does not climb the characteristic high ridge of the other Westside Trail options, it is a refreshing creekside stroll far from development. Other than the few lucky homeowners whose backyards melt into the trail, the route along Salt Creek is relatively natural and peaceful. It also avoids any challenging grades.

Begin the hike at a small gravel parking area on Lower Springs Road, where you will find a water faucet and not much else. Although you can park at CA 299, this parking area is much quieter and avoids the zooming traffic of the highway. The trail marker is very low-profile; look for a slim BLM marker across Lower Springs Road. The first steps of the hike immediately snake through a thick manzanita forest before a slight drop into Salt Creek's petite valley. Over the next mile the stroll skirts Salt Creek, which will only be pumping high volumes of water in late winter and early spring.

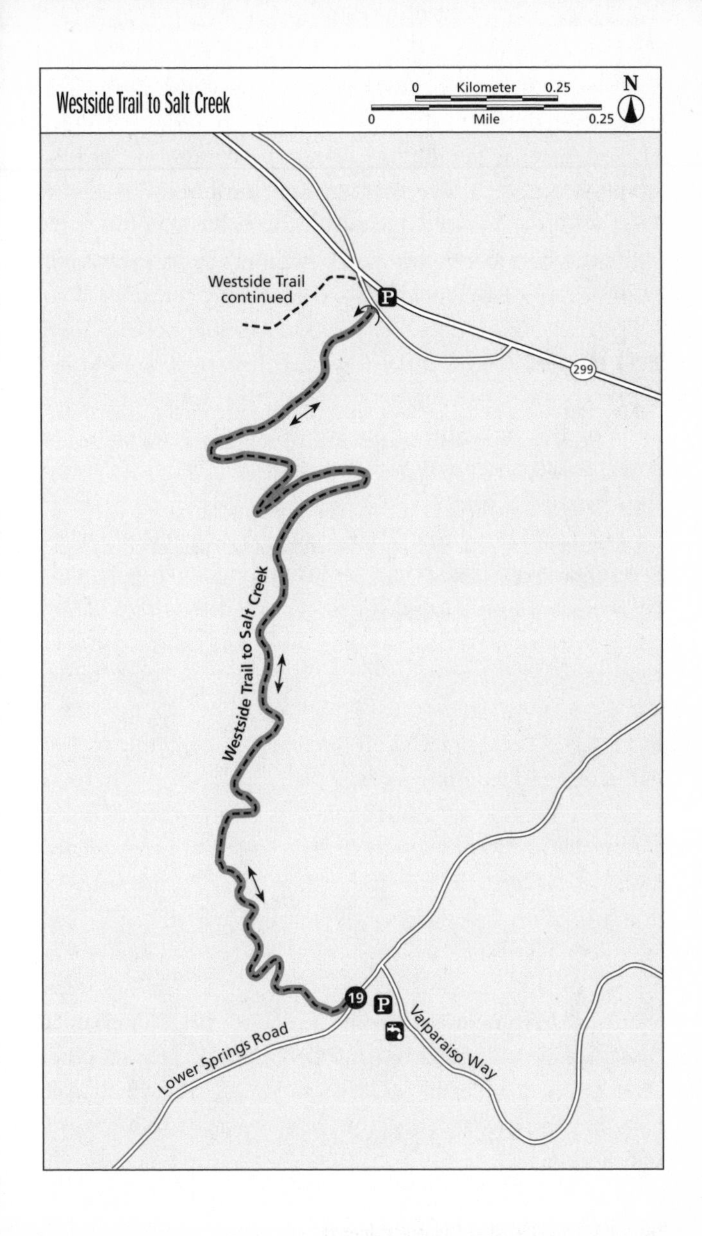
Westside Trail to Salt Creek
0
Kilometer
0.25
0
Mile
0.25
N
Westside Trail continued
P
299
Westside Trail to Salt Creek
19
P
Lower Springs Road
Valparaiso Way

After a couple of footbridges, the trail diverts from the creek and climbs an exposed hillside along a lengthy switchback. A short 0.5 mile leads to the other side of the hill, where you'll reach the highway. This is a good turnaround point for a short 3-mile round-trip hike, but you can continue to follow the trail as it cuts left and climbs a steep old roadbed to a rocky high ridge.

Miles and Directions

0.0 Beginning at the parking area, cautiously cross the road and look for the low-profile, brown BLM trail marker to the left and follow the trail northwest over a small hill.

1.1 Merge with an old road and continue straight.

1.5 End at CA 299. Backtrack from here or continue straight to extend your trip.

3.0 Arrive back at the trailhead.

20 Wintu Trail

Enticingly rugged, yet nearly urban, the Swasey Recreation Area is just a hop, skip, and a jump from central Redding, but it still manages to present all the best of the wilds. The Wintu Trail wanders through classic mixed hardwood forest, grassland chaparral, and manzanita groves as it climbs a muscle-moving hillside. Bring your dog, or your horse, and don't forget a sack lunch for the perfectly placed picnic area and million-dollar views.

Distance: 3-mile lollipop (with longer options)
Approximate hiking time: 1.5 hours
Difficulty: Moderate
Trail surface: Rock and dirt path
Best season: Year-round
Other trail users: Mountain bikers, equestrians
Canine compatibility: Leashed dogs permitted
Fees and permits: None
Schedule: None
Maps: TOPO! California CD, Disc 2; USGS Redding, CA; Bureau of Land Management's flyer: Swasey Recreation Area (available at the trailhead)
Trail contacts: Bureau of Land Management, Redding Field Office, 355 Hemsted Dr., Redding, CA 96002; (530) 224-2100; www.blm.gov/ca/redding
Special considerations: No water at the trailhead

Finding the trailhead: You'll find the Swasey Recreation Area just west of downtown Redding. From downtown Redding at I-5, head west on CA 299 exit west and follow it as it zig-zags through downtown for 7 miles and turn left (south) onto Swasey Drive. After 2.8 miles, turn right onto the gravel road at the sign for the Swasey Recreation Area. Drive 0.1 mile to the first trailhead on your right, at N40 33.206' / W122 28.520'. You will find restrooms but little else at the trailhead.

The Hike

The Swasey Recreation Area feels far from Redding, especially for practically being an urban hike. You'll never sense the suburbs looming nearby. True to the Bureau of Land Management spirit, the rugged routes are practical and less pristine than other area hikes, offering a little feel of the backcountry and open to any sort of nonmotorized travel. On a busy weekend, expect at least a dozen equestrians and another dozen mountain bikers making use of this system.

The Wintu Trail offers a steep ascent with a sweet reward. There are two ways to take this loop. Heading clockwise it will be a steady hike uphill for nearly 2 miles, but the elevation change is dispersed. Contrastingly, if you head counterclockwise, you'll put the ascent behind you in just a quick 0.5 mile and encounter the picnic area at the top of the climb. The lovely picnic area is not much more than a couple of tables in the shade of an overlook, but the inviting, nearly panoramic vistas include views of Mount Shasta, Lassen Peak, and Brokeoff Mountain. The vista point is worth a pause after climbing the switchbacks, even if a feast isn't in order. You might contemplate how the thoughtful touch of a couple of picnic tables got there, or why the trail was named Wintu, referring to the local Native Americans who once lived off this beautiful land.

Back on the trail, a more mellow hike over rolling hills awaits. The hike quickly climbs up a wonderful forest of knobcone and ponderosa pine, black and blue oak, as well as that tricky poison oak. On the chaparral slopes you'll come across whiteleaf manzanita, bedstraw, and buttonbush. The fairly high and dry rolling hilltop hike is thick in grasses,

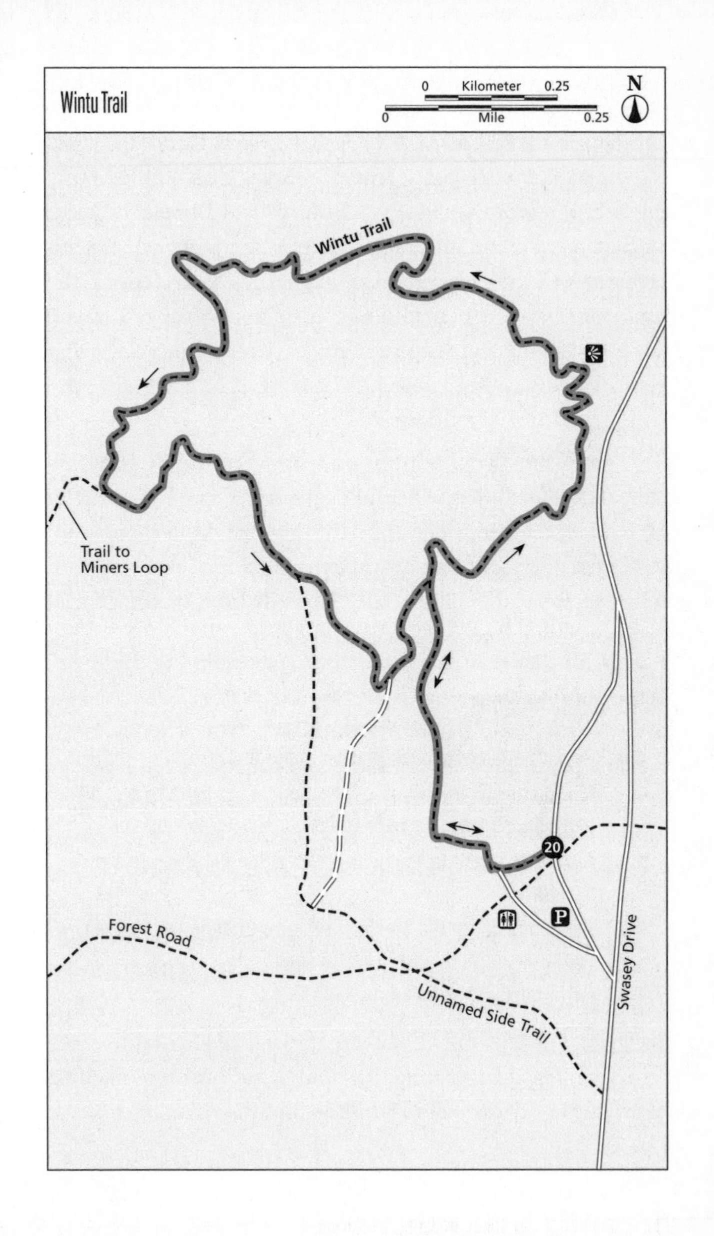
Wintu Trail
0
Kilometer
0.25
0
Mile
0.25
N
Wintu Trail
Trail to
Miners Loop
20
Forest Road
Unnamed Side Trail
Swasey Drive

with quaking grass, needlegrass, and wild oat blowing softly in the wind.

When the loop nears completion, it drops back down into the pines, away from the mountain views into some much needed shade. The occasional vetch, clover, spring beauty, and beautifully unique Tolmie star-tulip, which looks like a purple poppy with three fuzzy petals, bloom in spring. Pack the macro lens; this flower is a sight to behold. By mile 2.6 you meet back up with the lollipop portion of the hike and continue the out-and-back portion to the trailhead.

The Wintu Trail is only one route of the Swasey system. There are plenty of trails and open space waiting to be explored on another day. In fact, the Mule Mountain Pass Trail connects with Whiskeytown National Recreation Area. Stop by the BLM office or print one of the official maps online before you hit this extension.

Miles and Directions

0.0 Begin the out-and-back portion of the trail.

0.4 At the intersection with the loop portion, go right for a counterclockwise loop. There is steep but short elevation gain.

1.4 A small footpath to the right at top of the hill leads to a picnic area.

2.0 The connector to the Meiner Trail forks to the right; stay left on the main route for the Wintu Trail.

2.6 Arrive back at the lollipop.

3.0 Arrive back at the trailhead.

21 Clear Creek Greenway to Horsetown's Vista Point

The Clear Creek Greenway is a delightful series of rough routes in southwest Redding following Clear Creek and the surrounding hills. The 1.5-mile hike from the Horsetown Trailhead easily climbs to a lookout over the cavernous canyon of Clear Creek.

Distance: 3-mile out-and-back
Approximate hiking time: 1.5 hours
Difficulty: Easy
Trail surface: Dirt and rock path
Best season: Year-round
Other trail users: Mountain bikers, equestrians
Canine compatibility: Leashed dogs permitted
Fees and permits: None
Schedule: None
Maps: TOPO! California CD, Disc 3; USGS Redding, CA; Bureau of Land Management's flyer: Clear Creek Greenway (available online or at the Redding office); Shasta County Public Health Department's brochure: Redding Walks (available at BLM)
Trail contacts: Bureau of Land Management, Redding Field Office, 355 Hemsted Dr., Redding, CA 96002, (530) 224-2100, www.blm.gov/ca/redding; Horsetown–Clear Creek Preserve, (530) 241-2026
Special considerations: There are no facilities at this trailhead. This trail is fairly exposed and subject to extreme summer heat; if hiking during the hot summer months, consider traveling this route closer to dawn or dusk.

Finding the trailhead: From I-5 in central Redding, take the CA 299 exit west and carefully follow the signs for CA 273 South/Market Street as it zigzags through downtown. Follow 273 south 4.5 miles and turn left onto Clear Creek Road. There are several trailheads for the Clear Creek Greenway; the Horsetown Trailhead is on the right

6.5 miles down the road. The trail is across Clear Creek Road from the parking area, at N40 29.649' / W122 29.895'.

The Hike

Similar to its Westside Trail cousin, Clear Creek Greenway is another new and ever-changing system of beautiful backwoods routes created from a conglomerate of public land and a cooperative effort of several organizations. The Clear Creek Greenway stretches from CA 273 west to the old Saeltzer Dam and Cloverdale Road. Many will wonder, what dam? The now-defunct reservoir once hosted a dam that was removed in 2000 to make way for natural-habitat reclamation.

The restoration and preservation of Clear Creek's watershed had been a long time coming, and the environment has shed its share of tears prior to the project. If you extend your hike to incorporate a lengthier walk along Clear Creek, you might notice the numerous dredge tailings piles. Though time has mellowed their stature and plants have dug roots into the rocky mounds, these are the remnants of the gold rush that once pumped the precious gravels out of the water and milked them for gold. The status of Clear Creek has come full circle from the mining craze. Today you can view healthy salmon populations swimming in the placid stream, and if you're here in fall, be sure to check out the spawning beds from the fish platforms at the main overlook.

This detailed portion of the Clear Creek Greenway system leads from the Horsetown Trailhead to a vista point on the brink of Clear Creek Canyon. At the narrow, rocky canyon, keep an eye peeled for osprey, turkey vulture, and bald eagle. The short hike flows along open hillsides on an earthen single-track path. The name of the trailhead refers

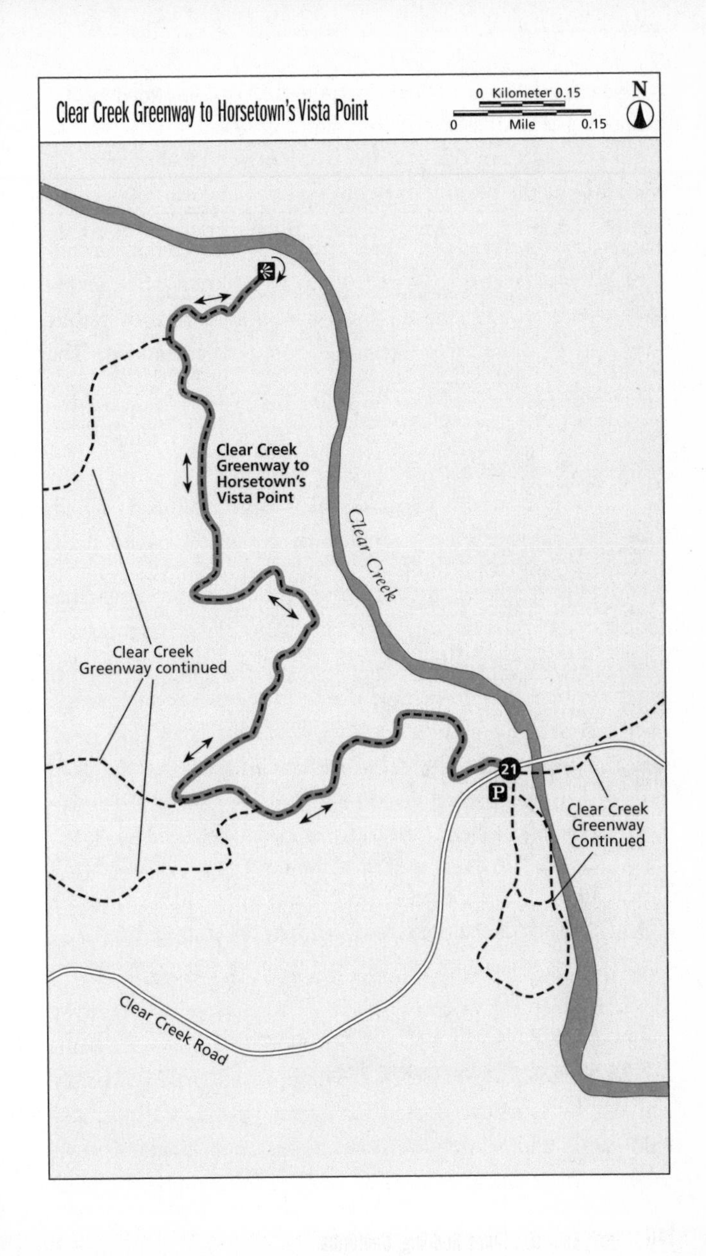
Clear Creek Greenway to Horsetown's Vista Point
0 Kilometer 0.15
0 Mile 0.15
N
Clear Creek Greenway to Horsetown's Vista Point
Clear Creek
Clear Creek Greenway continued
21
P
Clear Creek Greenway Continued
Clear Creek Road

to Horsetown, a circa-1850s gold-rush town said to have had upward of a dozen saloons but only about 1,000 people. After the gold ran out and the town burned twice, nothing remains but the testament of tailing piles. As you hike in this historic area, try to envision life and the ravaged environment of nearly a century ago.

This hike is just one spur of the dozen miles of possible journeys along the Clear Creek Greenway. If you'd like to extend your day hike, think about choosing a contrasting scene from the overlook. Wander back down toward the parking area to head east along Clear Creek, where you will pass those telltale tailing piles and get an up-close view of the salmon at the Clear Creek Gorge trailhead, which features a salmon viewing platform as well as paved paths and restrooms. Managed in a cooperative effort with the Horsetown–Clear Creek Nature Preserve, Clear Creek Greenway hosts many events, from GPS navigation classes to naturalist- and historian-led hikes. Contact the BLM for more information.

Miles and Directions

0.0 From the trailhead, carefully cross Clear Creek Road and follow the slim brown BLM trail marker north onto the Cloverdale Trail.

0.3 Stay right at the intersection with Piety Hill Loop.

1.3 A side trail merges with the main trail here. Head right for the vista point.

1.5 Arrive at the vista point. Backtrack from here.

3.0 Arrive back at the parking area.

22 Hog Lake Plateau

This unparalleled spring beauty just north of Red Bluff bursts in a mosaic of wildflowers. This loosely maintained Bureau of Land Management area is home to a crosshatch of unofficial little routes, but the Hog Lake Plateau Trail is easily distinguished as it leads from Hog Lake to the Paynes Creek Wetlands.

Distance: 7.5-mile out-and-back
Approximate hiking time: 4 hours
Difficulty: Easy
Trail surface: Rough dirt and rock roadbed
Best season: Spring
Other trail users: Mountain bikers, equestrians, hunters
Canine compatibility: Leashed dogs permitted
Fees and permits: None
Schedule: None
Maps: TOPO! California CD, Disc 3; USGS Bend, CA; Bureau of Land Management's flyer: *Sacramento River Bend Area Guide* (available at BLM)
Trail contacts: Bureau of Land Management, Redding Field Office, 355 Hemsted Dr., Redding, CA 96002; (530) 224-2100; www.blm.gov/ca/redding
Special considerations: There are no facilities at this trailhead. Hog Lake Plateau is actively leased to ranchers whose cattle roam the property. It is possible for cows to be on the trail. This trail is fairly exposed and subject to extreme summer heat. If hiking during the hot summer months, consider taking this route closer to dawn or dusk.

Finding the trailhead: From Redding head south on I-5 for 30 miles and take the CA 36/99–Antelope Road exit east. Drive 2 miles and turn left onto CA 36. The trailhead is on your left after 7.3 miles (past the similarly labeled Iron Mountain Trailhead), at N40 16.772' / W122 07.304'.

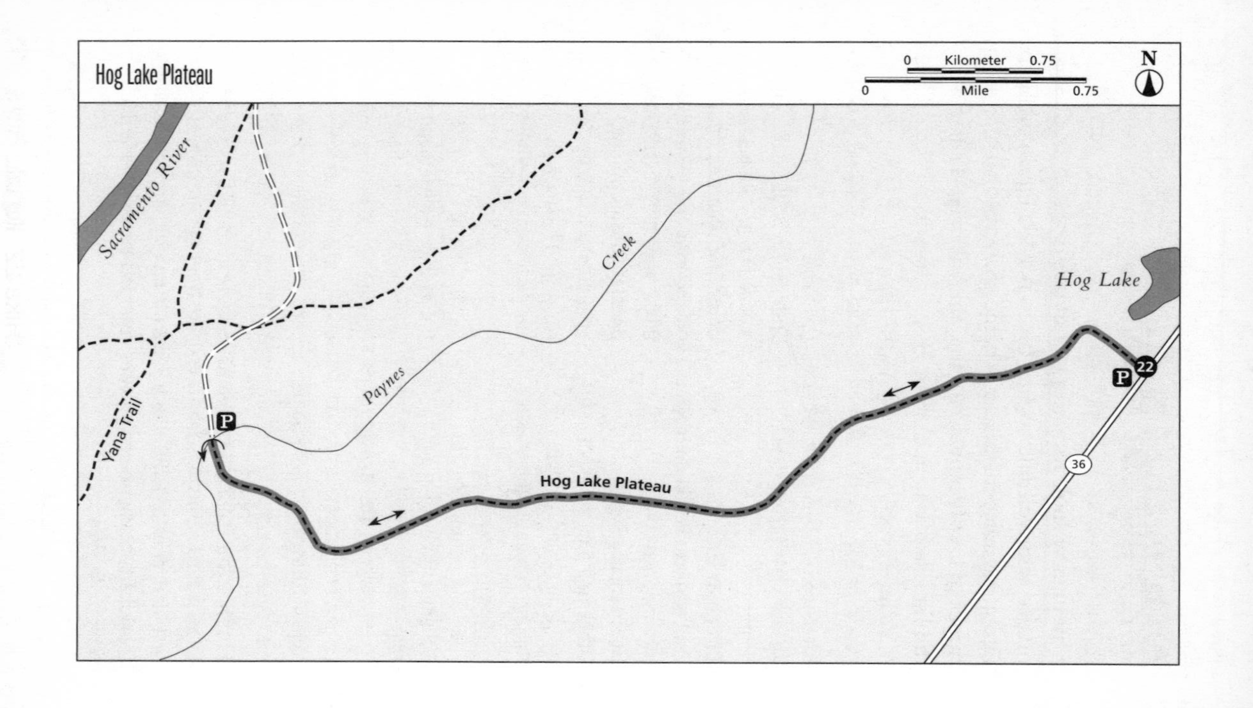
Hog Lake Plateau
0 Kilometer 0.75
0 Mile 0.75
N
Sacramento River
Creek
Paynes
Hog Lake
Yana Trail
P
Hog Lake Plateau
36
P
22

The Hike

If you arrive at any other time than spring, Hog Lake Plateau may look like nothing more than a dry cow field riddled with volcanic rubble, but when the dustbowl ripens into a magnificent seasonal wetland, complete with a showy carpet of low-lying wildflowers, this hike should be first on the list.

The Paynes Creek Wetlands is part of the protected block of Sacramento River riparian zone, a valuable habitat along the river's edge, although you will not see the river on this particular trail. Instead, this route begins off CA 36 a few miles north of Red Bluff and travels west to Paynes Creek, a short 0.5 mile or so before the Sacramento River.

As you take your first steps along the trail, Hog Lake is on your immediate right. In spring, this wide, shallow lake fans out into a large body. As the lake recedes, wildflowers band the edges of the pool in rings of meadowfoam, California goldfield, buttercup, succulent owl's clover, violet, milkmaid, lupine, and clover. Later in the year, the lake shrivels into little more than a mucky cow trough.

Wildlife, too, finds habitat on the preserve's trails. Numerous birds, as well as spunky jackrabbits and the impressively strong population of deer, pass through this preserve. Coyotes and bobcats also survive off this land. Look for the western fence lizard scurrying about on the andesite boulders. The lizard is the hiker's friend in that it is responsible for keeping local ticks low in Lyme disease. (The lizard's unique chemistry neutralizes the potent disease when it is bitten by a tick.) Identified by their bright blue stomachs, they are sometimes referred to as blue bellies.

The exposed trail leads to gusty fronts on the plateau before dropping down to Paynes Creek. It also presents spectacular mountain views. In spring, when the warm sun heats your face despite the chilly breeze, you can look across a green blanket of grass sprinkled with blue oaks and wildflowers beneath the snowcapped peaks of such greats as Lassen Peak and Brokeoff Mountain to the east, and unmistakable Black Butte to the north. The only downside to a visit during the wetter months is that Paynes Creek quickly becomes impassable with a little rainfall, so you will have to end your journey 0.1 mile shy of the Paynes Creek Crossing Trailhead.

Miles and Directions

0.0 Beginning at the Hog Lake Plateau Trailhead, head northwest from the parking area. Hog Lake is a couple hundred yards away on your right.

0.2 There is a small cattle trail to the right. Stay left for Hog Lake Plateau.

3.5 Reach a gate. Always close the gate behind you.

3.6 Cross Paynes Creek. This creek may be impassable in the wetter months; if you are unsure of the crossing, do not attempt it.

3.7 Reach the Paynes Creek Crossing Trailhead. Backtrack from here.

7.5 Arrive back at the Hog Lake Plateau Trailhead.

23 Yana Trail

Much like Hog Lake Plateau, the Yana Trail is a terminus of Paynes Creek and a seasonal wonder when wildflowers bloom. The grasslands blossom in a pastel mélange of yellow, pink, and blue wildflowers. The short loop around Bass Pond circles a woodland rich in vernal pools, awash in seasonal beauty and flooded with life during spring. The seasonal ponds that dot this trail may only host water for a couple short months, but during that time a multitude of migratory birds utilize the grounds for staging and nesting areas.

Distance: 2.5-mile loop (with longer options)
Approximate hiking time: 1.5 hours
Difficulty: Easy
Trail surface: Dirt and rock path
Best season: Spring
Other trail users: Mountain bikers, equestrians, hunters
Canine compatibility: Leashed dogs permitted
Fees and permits: None
Schedule: None
Maps: TOPO! California CD, Disc 3; USGS Bend, CA; Bureau of Land Management's flyer: *Sacramento River Bend Area Guide* (available at BLM)
Trail contacts: Bureau of Land Management, Redding Field Office, 355 Hemsted Dr., Redding, CA 96002; (530) 224-2100; www.blm.gov/ca/redding
Special considerations: No water at the trailhead

Finding the trailhead: From Redding take I-5 south for 27 miles, then take the Jellys Ferry Road exit east. Drive 2.5 miles and turn right onto Bend Ferry Road. Continue for 2.6 miles (passing the school) to the trailhead, on the left, at N40 16.300' / W122 11.827'.

The Hike

Also a short drive from Red Bluff, the Yana Trail is located across Paynes Creek from Hog Lake Plateau, and although it has to be accessed from a separate freeway exit, the two trails are part of the same contiguous 3,700-acre Paynes Creek Wetlands. The Yana Trail is a very popular equestrian route and totals 8 rolling miles through blue oak grasslands aside the Sacramento River. Roughly midway, a primitive camp located at Massacre Flat is popular with backpackers and trail riders.

For a nice introduction to the lengthy Yana Trail, begin on this easy loopside Bass Pond. The loop begins at the Bass Pond Trailhead, the most well developed of the Yana Trail's trio of trailheads. Follow the trail north from the restrooms through an open meadow thick in tall grasses. When the trail enters the grove of beautiful blue oaks, a left at the Y intersection will take hikers along a ridge overlooking the Sacramento River. The divide merges again a quick 0.25 mile later. Many social trails also fork from the loop; when in doubt, try to follow the most well-used footpath. After a couple of gentle hills, the loop will cross and follow a gravel road up to the trail's continuation on the right behind a rusted gate. After the road crossing, you enter another meadow rich in vernal pools and seasonal wetlands.

In spring, when the grounds are sopping with seasonal rains, fruitful wildflower blooms are a real treat. This is also the time of year neotropical migratory birds stop here on their journey north. The Redding and Red Bluff region is located on the Pacific Flyway. If you've ever had any interest in birds, it is likely that you've heard of the Pacific Flyway—the great route of migratory waterfowl stretching

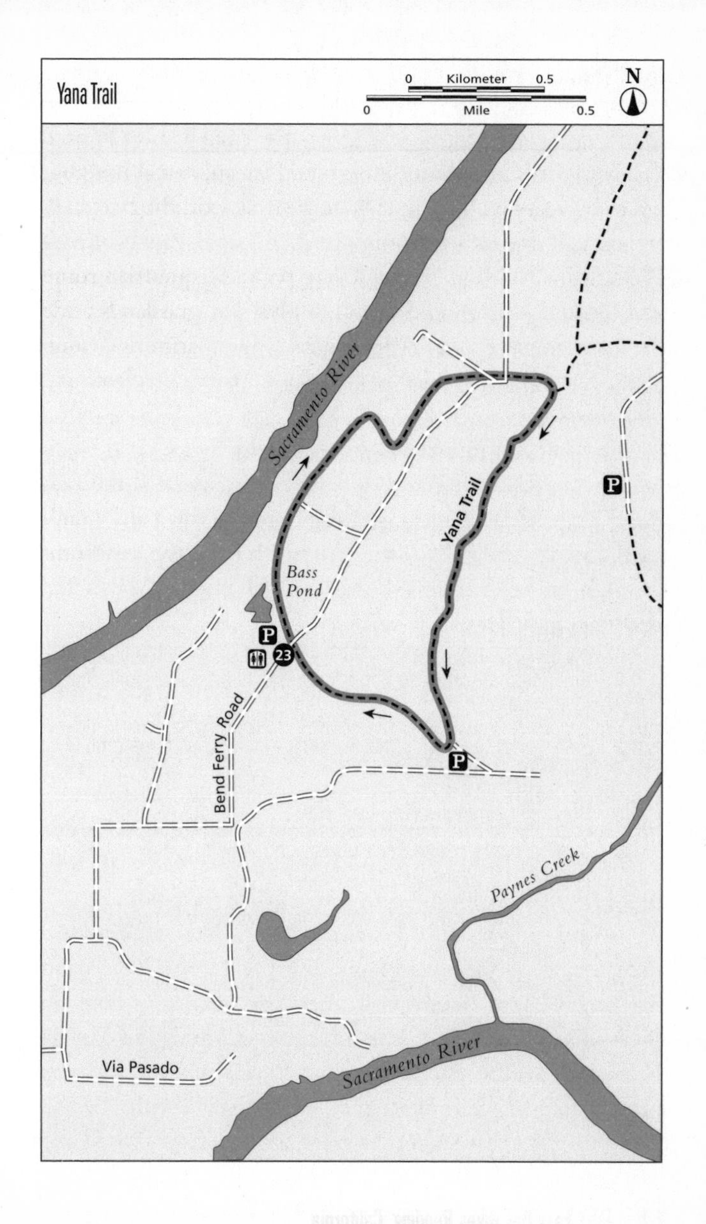
Yana Trail
0
Kilometer
0.5
0
Mile
0.5
N
Sacramento River
Yana Trail
Bass
Pond
P
23
Bend Ferry Road
P
P
Paynes Creek
Sacramento River
Via Pasado

from South America to Alaska. Redding offers hikers the reward of being tucked into this course on the northernmost end of the California's Central Valley, a bowl known for producing priceless habitat. This diminishing environment is an increasing problem for these valiant Flyway birds, so it is no surprise that this small field hosts so much life at special times of year. Full of people or not, the birds will take advantage of these hard-to-come-by vernal pools.

Keep an eye out within the marshy grasses for such classics as American coot and widgeon, common moorhen, green-winged teal, and Northern pintail. Better yet, bring a birding guide and a set of binoculars. The best time to view wildlife on this preserve is at sunrise. Not only are people more scarce, but animals are more active toward dawn and dusk.

Miles and Directions

0.0 Beginning at the Bass Pond Trailhead, head north along the Yana Trail.

0.2 Stay left at the Y to follow the trail, which has Sacramento River views here.

0.6 Stay right at another Y intersection.

1.0 Carefully cross Bend Ferry Road and follow the intersecting unlabeled gravel road for 0.1 mile.

1.1 Exit the road to the right, following the rough trail behind the BLM gate.

2.0 Stay right at the Y intersection and circle seasonal wetlands.

2.5 Cross back over Bend Ferry Road and arrive back at the trailhead.

Clubs and Trail Groups

Healthy Shasta
2660 Breslauer Way
Redding, CA 96001
(530) 229-8243
www.healthyshasta.org

Pacific Crest Trail Association
1331 Garden Highway
Sacramento, CA 95833
(916) 285-1846
www.pcta.org

Sierra Club Shasta Group
P.O. Box 491554
Redding, CA 96049
National Headquarters: (415) 977-5500
www.sierraclub.org / http://motherlode.sierraclub.org/shasta

Wintu Audubon Society
www.wintuaudubon.org